STEP-BY-STEP GUIDE TO

DOG CARE

PRACTICAL ADVICE ON FEEDING, GROOMING, BREEDING, TRAINING, HEALTH CARE AND FIRST AID, WITH MORE THAN 300 PHOTOGRAPHS

DR PETER LARKIN

PHOTOGRAPHY BY JOHN DANIELS

southwater

This edition is published by Southwater
an imprint of Anness Publishing Ltd
Blaby Road, Wigston, Leicestershire LE18 4SE
info@anness.com

www.southwaterbooks.com; www.annesspublishing.com

If you like the images in this book and would like to investigate
using them for publishing, promotions or advertising, please visit
our website www.practicalpictures.com for more information.

A CIP catalogue record for this book is available from the British Library.

Publisher: Joanna Lorenz
Editor: Fiona Eaton
Editorial Assistant: Emma Gray
Photography: John Daniels
Additional Photography: Jane Burton pp94, 95
Designer: Michael Morey
Production Controller: Mai-Ling Collyer

Previously published as part of a larger volume, *The Complete Dog Book*

PUBLISHER'S NOTE
Although the advice and information in this book are believed
to be accurate and true at the time of going to press, neither the
authors nor the publisher can accept any legal responsibility or
liability for any errors or omissions that may have been made nor
for any inaccuracies nor for any loss, harm or injury that comes
about from following instructions or advice in this book.

Contents

INTRODUCTION

The dog is humanity's oldest companion. Human and dog came together thousands of years ago for mutual comfort and slowly developed the interdependence seen today – human's caring for the dog in return for continuing companionship and a great variety of working functions.

The gradual recognition of the many different ways in which the dog could contribute to the association has led to the development of an enormous variety of dog types. All varieties of dog are members of a single species; it is the most varied of any species known, ranging from the tiny Chihuahua to the massive Irish Wolfhound.

So close has the association of dog and human become that there are now probably only two breeds of truly wild dogs left, the Cape Hunting Dog and the Australian Dingo. Many countries,

✦ RIGHT
The Golden Retriever is one of the most popular companion breeds and has an impeccable working background as a gundog.

of course, have roaming packs of wild dogs that lead an independent existence, but these are invariably domestic dogs that have "gone wild" for one of any number of reasons.

To a remarkable extent, a dog of any breed can mate with another of any other breed and produce fertile offspring. This fact in itself has led to even more varieties developing over the centuries, as new functions and

fashions were thought up. There are something like four hundred known breeds in existence today. The precise figure is impossible to determine as previously unrecognized breeds continue to emerge, and types of the same breed are recognized as distinct; or conversely, varieties previously

✦ BELOW
This German Shepherd is a true companion and guard, always keen to please his owner.

✦ ABOVE
Dogs are inveterate game-players, always learning from their play.

✦ RIGHT
Dogs may learn to carry out all kinds of helpful tasks, including collecting and delivering items around the house.

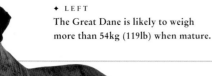

◆ LEFT
The Great Dane is likely to weigh
more than 54kg (119lb) when mature.

◆ LEFT
A dog will roll on to
its back as a sign of
submission to its
owner or to another
dog.

considered as separate are combined
as one breed.

As part of this continuing
evolutionary process, breeds have
also died out; several have disappeared
even in the last one hundred years,
possibly due to reduced fertility or
the particular type ceasing to be
fashionable. Loss of the traditional
function of a breed may be another
reason, but more often the breed has
changed in conformation to such an
extent as to be almost unrecognizable
as the original breed. The war dogs of
old, for instance, have developed into
the civilized mastiff types.

Although every breed of dog, in
the western world at least, is expected
to be domesticated, certain type
characteristics tend to persist through
many generations, and these are not
just characteristics of conformation.
Everyone realizes that if you buy a
Great Dane puppy, for instance,
small though it may be at eight weeks
old, it will grow into a very large dog.
If you buy a terrier of whatever breed,

it will have terrier behaviour
characteristics, inherited from its
working ancestors.

If you have decided to buy a dog,
look into all the breed characteristics,
and consider them carefully before
you decide which type of dog you
want to live with. A dog may live for
between ten and twenty years – it is
yours to care for over a good part of
your life.

◆ LEFT
The young of every
breed are appealing,
but an owner's
responsibility may
last for over fifteen
years.

◆ RIGHT
Children and dogs
are good for each
other. Both have
much to learn from
their mutual love.

Choosing a Suitable Dog

Many households are just not suitable for a dog. If you work long periods away from home, or even just very long hours, and if there is no-one else at home while you are away, you need to consider very carefully whether the comforts of coming home to a dog are not outweighed by the lack of company that the dog will have to endure, with all the potential behaviour problems that this may cause. Consider not just how the dog would fit into your own way of life, but how your lifestyle would affect the dog.

◆ FACING PAGE
Before getting a dog, it is important to ensure that you can provide it with the environment it needs.

WHAT TYPE OF DOG?

◆ BELOW
Dogs enjoy the companionship of other dogs, with some surprising friendships.

Dogs are companions. If you want one just as a guard, buy a burglar alarm. Dogs are usually effective burglar deterrents, whatever their breed, but their first function in a home must be as a friend – and there is no better friend. They don't criticize you (or not too unkindly), they don't sulk (or not for too long), and they are always there to comfort you and love you.

Choosing the right breed is an intensely personal matter, but there are broad guidelines.

The size of the fully grown dog is important, but perhaps not quite so critical as it may seem. Very large dogs need a lot of exercise, and once you have decided that there is room in your house for a large dog, exercise is the most important consideration. Most people, however, want a dog that fits reasonably into the home environment. A couple of Wolfhounds may be your ideal, but their bulk may make a small flat uninhabitable.

The Labrador Retriever, a dog which, if not overweight, will weigh when mature about 30kg (66lb), is the most popular dog in the United States and the United Kingdom, with 132,000 in the US and 32,000 in the UK. Second in the US is the Rottweiler, with almost 94,000 registered, and

◆ FACING
A common problem with insecure dogs is barking when they are left alone. Once established it may be very difficult to overcome.

◆ LEFT
Complete family integration with people and dogs all joining in as many activities as possible will usually prevent behaviour problems.

◆ LEFT
Most dogs love
jumping for toys. It
can be a helpful
supplement to their
exercise when walks
are restricted.

◆ BELOW
Some breeds, like the Border Collie,
spend hours looking for attention.
Ignore them at your peril!

third the German Shepherd with 79,000 registered. In Britain the German Shepherd is second (24,000) and the Golden Retriever third (16,000). These are all large dogs. By no means do all of them live in large houses.

Breed or type behaviour is probably more important in choosing a dog than any other characteristic. It pays to ask not just dedicated owners but knowledgeable people outside the breed – your veterinary surgeon sees a wide variety of dogs every day.

Typically, the terrier types are lively, not easy to train, but very responsive dogs. They are good with children if properly trained.

Toy dogs are usually better companions for owners who do not have young children. The dogs may be upset by what they perceive as large noisy humans rushing around. Their fear may make them snappy, with unhappy results. All toy dogs will be happy with as much exercise as you can give them, but they may be equally happy with only a moderate amount.

Hounds need as much exercise as possible. With this condition they make very good house dogs who love their comfort. Breeds in the other groups vary, but, in general, the working breeds are all better with an occupation that keeps them out of mischief.

The gundog (sporting) breeds are generally easy to train, and settle into the human environment without difficulty. They need exercise, and lack of exercise shows!

Certain of the herding breeds, typified by the Border Collie, are, or should be regarded as, specialist working dogs. They demand more attention than other breeds if they are not to become neurotic pets. Outside their traditional working function they have become the outstanding type in obedience work of all sorts. Provided you are able to give sufficient attention to them to keep their very active minds occupied, they are among the most rewarding of pets. But if you don't, they will find something to occupy themselves, and it will be trouble.

With so many breeds to choose from, as well as crossbreds and mongrels, there really isn't a typical household pet these days.

◆ RIGHT
This charming
Bernese puppy will
make a beautiful
house pet, but he
will grow to 70 cm
(27½ in) at the
shoulder when
mature.

THE COST OF KEEPING A DOG

Can you afford it? Buying a dog is the start. Very few puppies can be acquired for nothing. Almost everyone will want to sell the litter they have reared, even if only to try to recoup the cost of feeding the puppies to weaning.

The cost of good pedigree puppies varies from country to country. In the United Kingdom, depending on breed, a puppy may cost from around £300, although probably the average price asked for a well-bred puppy of most breeds is between £400 and £600. In the United States asking prices are usually somewhat higher, from about $1,000 upwards. Australian prices are similar to those in the United Kingdom. Imported puppies in any country may cost a great deal more.

The initial examination by the veterinary surgeon, and the puppy's primary inoculations will be around another £30, perhaps $60 in the United States, and you can spend as much as you wish on toys and equipment.

A substantial part of the cost of keeping a dog may be the cost of veterinary treatment. Veterinary surgeons are these days capable of sophisticated treatments of illness or injury, but they have no subsidy for the costs. If your dog ever needs complicated or prolonged veterinary treatment the cost may be high.

There are several pet insurance companies catering for veterinary treatments; each has its own approach, and dog owners would be well advised to study what each company offers before deciding which policy to buy.

✦ BELOW
Diet and exercise may both be critical to the well-being of the older dog. Overweight dogs are often reluctant to walk far; a few pounds off works wonders.

✦ RIGHT
The size and breed of a dog may not be an accurate guide to its demand for exercise.

The premium grade policies offer sums for the death of your dog, and for rewards to be offered if the dog is lost. They may include kennelling fees in case of your own illness, even holiday cancellation costs. The level of veterinary fees covered is variable on most schemes, and it may be worth discussing this with your veterinary surgeon. All additions cost money.

Some companies will offer a basic veterinary fee insurance as an alternative to the premium schemes. It will be up to you to decide which of the various forms of insurance best fits your own needs.

Most insurers offer a puppy scheme, sometimes with an incentive to transfer to the adult scheme when it expires. Many breeders will offer puppy insurance to buyers, either as part of or as an extra cost to the purchase price of the puppy.

Feeding costs vary greatly. In theory, the smaller the dog, the less expensive to feed, but this is frequently offset by choosing more specialized, and therefore expensive, foods for the very small pet. It is possible to feed a 14kg (31lb) dog very adequately for about £3.50 ($6.00) a week.

✦ ABOVE
Running with a companion dog is terrific exercise, but be sure you are in control.

✦ LEFT
Diets to rear healthy puppies need careful consideration. The breeder will usually offer sound advice, but be wary of bizarre feeding regimes.

PEDIGREE OR NON-PEDIGREE

◆ LEFT
If you choose a pedigree dog, you must still look for a strain in that breed that fits your lifestyle. Gundogs (sporting) can come from a "working" or a "show" strain.

Crossbred dogs, the most identifiable of which is the Lurcher, are usually not expensive to buy, which is an obvious advantage. They have their own "mutt" charm, and their apparent type may be just what you are looking for. But remember the tiny puppy may become an enormous adult. The best way to judge is to see both parents, but in the nature of things the father is likely to be "away on business" when the puppies are ready to leave.

It is not necessarily true that crossbred dogs are healthier than purebreds, as many people believe. Every veterinary surgeon can tell you of crossbreds or mongrels suffering from recognizable, inherited diseases.

The advantage of picking a purebred dog is that you know what you are getting. From a reputable breeder a Cocker Spaniel puppy will grow up into a Cocker Spaniel dog, of a size and weight that is within the breed norm, and with potential behaviour characteristics typical of the breed. There is, or should be, advice available to deal with whatever problems may arise as a particular feature of the breed.

There is no doubt that many breeds have inherited problems associated with that breed, although these have often been exaggerated in the press. It is up to the potential owner to enquire about these problems, and to take independent advice on their significance. It is worth bearing in mind that no species of animal, including human beings, is free from inheritable disease. Dogs may be less afflicted than most.

◆ LEFT
A lovable mongrel. Did his owners know how he was going to turn out? And have they the time and inclination to give that coat the attention it demands?

◆ RIGHT
Crossbred dogs are often the basis for new working types. A cross between two recognized breeds is likely to have characteristics somewhere between the two.

DOG OR BITCH

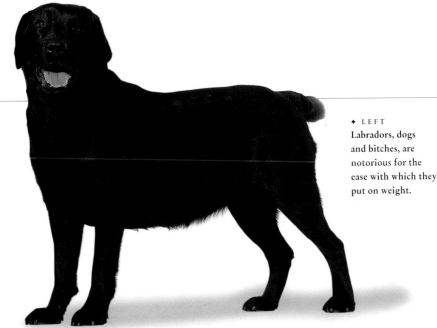

Choosing whether to have a male or female – a dog or a bitch – is one of the early decisions.

Dogs tend to have a more "macho" outlook on life than bitches, and if that attracts you, the male of the species will be your choice. Dogs are

♦ RIGHT
The King Charles Spaniel is regarded by many as the ideal family pet.

possibly more outgoing, certainly on average a little harder to train, but often more responsive once trained.

They do not, of course, come into season twice a year, with the attendant bother of oestrous discharges, and the attraction of all the dogs in the neighbourhood. But don't forget that

it is the male dogs that are attracted, and if you have a male it could be yours that has to be dragged home each night from his wanderings.

On balance, if there is such a thing in this particular choice, the female is likely to make a better family pet. She is less likely to be aggressive, although dominance is as much a breed characteristic as it is related to the sex of the dog. Bitches are much less likely to try to wander for most of the year, and they are inclined to be more loving to their human family.

♦ LEFT
Labradors, dogs and bitches, are notorious for the ease with which they put on weight.

♦ BELOW
The Boston Terrier needs the minimum of grooming but likes its exercise.

♦ LEFT
The Rough Collie is a working dog; not for the lazy owner.

♦ FAR LEFT
The Airedale is a real terrier in every respect.

♦ BELOW
The Dachshund is a well-loved breed.

BUYING A PUPPY

Let us assume that you know more or less the type of dog you feel you can best live with. Even though you may have no intention of ever showing your dog, dog shows are good places to visit while you are finally making up your mind. Talk to the people showing, find out what their views are about their breed – you may find that many of the exhibitors are remarkably frank about the drawbacks as well as the virtues of their breed. In the long run it pays them to be so.

The next step is to look for the right breeder, not necessarily the top one in the breed, who would, quite fairly, expect a premium price for puppies of show standard. Top breeders, however, will often be the most genuinely encouraging to the potential new owner.

Many dogs are still sold through so-called "puppy farms" and pet shops. Neither is a suitable place to find a puppy. Young dogs cannot be treated as commodities to be traded at the convenience of their breeder, and serious health problems regularly arise from this form of mistreatment of young animals.

Take your time, and be prepared to wait to get the dog you really want. Above all, visit the kennels and make sure you see the dam with the puppies in the litter (and other litters), and, if possible, the sire. Make your own mind up about the conditions in which the puppies have been reared.

There is some argument about the right age to buy a puppy, although the general consensus seems to be that about eight weeks is right. Much before that may be too early to remove the puppy from the nest; leaving it later can give rise to socialization problems, with the time between six and eight weeks regarded by behaviourists as a critical period in the puppy's development. Certainly, if the puppy is much older than eight weeks, you need to be satisfied that it

◆ RIGHT
It is safe to let prospective owners handle the puppies if they haven't been handling other dogs.

◆ BELOW RIGHT
Retrievers tend to have very large litters, often ten or more. Weaning can start as early as three weeks with suitable supplements.

You may be expected to sign a contract setting out the limitations of the breeder's liability in the event of the puppy later developing an inheritable condition. We live in a litigious society. Recent court cases have made it plain that if a breeder fails to warn a purchaser of conditions that are recognized in the breed, and the puppy later develops such a condition, the breeder may be held liable, even though he or she is unaware of the existence of the problem in that puppy, and has taken reasonable precautions to avoid the condition.

The contract you may be asked to sign must be reasonable, and it is likely to consist of a statement drawing your attention to the known inheritable diseases of the breed and an expectation that you will have discussed the significance of the condition with your veterinary surgeon. Your veterinary surgeon may be advised to make his comments in a written statement.

has been exposed to a sensible social environment and not simply left in its rearing kennel to make its own way.

Be honest with the breeder. If you are looking for a dog that you may later want to show, don't pretend that you are only looking for a pet puppy, in the hope that the price might be lower. Explain truthfully and carefully the life that the puppy will lead, especially its home environment. At worst, the breeder will explain why that may not be suitable for rearing a puppy; at best, you may get much good advice.

Never expect a guarantee that your puppy will be a show winner. Even though it comes from the very best show stock, with a pedigree as long as your arm, no-one, including the most experienced breeders, can pick a "cert" at eight weeks.

The breeder should provide you with the puppy's pedigree, and a receipt for its purchase. If the breeder has already taken the puppies for their first inoculation, this may be included in the quoted price or regarded as an extra. You should ask.

◆ BELOW LEFT
The best way to decide on the suitability of
a particular kennel is to see as many of their
dogs as possible, both at home and at work
or in the show-ring.

◆ BELOW RIGHT
Ex-racing greyhounds make wonderful pets,
but occasionally have problems socializing
after years in a racing kennel.

The breeder should always provide you with a feeding chart for the next stage of rearing your puppy. It is worthwhile taking this to discuss with the veterinary surgeon when you take the puppy for its first visit. Many breeders give the new owner some sample feed to start the puppy off in its new home.

You should expect a healthy puppy, which has been wormed adequately, probably twice, and is free from skin parasites such as fleas or lice.

Pet insurance companies have short-term cover schemes, available to breeders for issue to new owners. Ask the breeder if he or she has such cover. If not, arrange your own as soon as you have bought the puppy. Puppies are at their most vulnerable during the first few weeks in their new homes.

◆ LEFT
The age to leave
home is a
compromise.
A critical
socializing time
is about six
weeks, when
ideally the puppy
should meet its
new family, but
other factors
usually dictate
that eight weeks
is probably the
best practical age
at which to buy
your puppy.

CHOOSING A PUPPY

Never be fobbed off with excuses about the condition a puppy is in or its behaviour; and never buy a puppy because it's the last one left and you feel sorry for it.

It is often said that puppies choose their new owners, rather than the other way around, and there is much truth to this claim. An overly shy puppy may have socialization problems later, and the puppy that comes forward from the nest, asking to be chosen, is probably the right one.

The puppy must be alert and have bright, clean eyes. Its nose must be clean (but forgive a little crust of food), its ears must be free of wax, and its coat must be clean and pleasant to handle and smell. There must be no sign of sores or grittiness on the skin and coat. Black "coal dust" is usually flea dirt – fleas themselves are more difficult to spot. Examine all the puppies briefly to ensure that they have been well cared for.

Make sure there is no discharge from the eyes. Forgive a scratch or two on the face – puppies in the nest don't always agree.

The membranes of the nose must be clear and free of discharge. There must be no sign of a runny nose.

The inside of the ears must look pink and shiny, without inflammation or dark-coloured wax. It should not look sore.

Soreness or inflammation of the rims of the eyes, or eyes that are not completely clear, may be serious signs of present or potential disease.

The puppy's coat and skin should feel loose and soft. The skin should be free of sores.

Sturdy, strong limbs are a must for any breed, although if you fancy an Italian Greyhound don't expect him to be this sturdy.

Puppies should have a clean bottom. Signs of diarrhoea are obvious from a quick examination behind. The whole litter should be examined.

17

SETTLING IN

Bringing home a new puppy or even an older dog is an important family occasion. Everyone wants to touch, hold and stroke the new member of the family, especially the children. But do take things slowly.

In the case of a puppy, this will be the first time away from the only environment the puppy has known, and away from his mother and litter mates. The world is huge and frightening. For an older dog, there is still a lot of adjusting for him to do.

Bring him home when there are not too many people around, and introduce him to his new environment in as relaxed a manner as possible. Let him look and sniff around, offer him a little something to eat, which he probably won't accept, and allow him to have a run around the garden. Bring your family and friends to meet the dog one or two at a time, and give him time to make friends before introducing anyone else.

◆ **LEFT**
Puppies' curiosity about new toys helps to overcome their awe of strange surroundings.

At some stage you have to cause a little more trauma by taking the dog to the veterinary surgeon for a health check. If at all possible, take him to the vet on the way home from the breeder or kennels. If there should be a problem that necessitates returning the dog to the seller (fortunately, a very rare occurrence), it is going to be much easier if the family haven't met and already fallen in love with him.

Once the settling in process has begun, interrupt the dog's established routine as little as possible. For a puppy, follow the breeder's feeding regime, giving the same number of feeds at the same time each day. To start with, give the food the dog is used to – the seller might have provided a "starter pack" – even if you have decided eventually to use a different type of food. Make any dietary changes gradually.

Clean water should always be available; show the dog where it is. Make sure that not only is the water bowl always full, but that it is washed regularly – dogs are messy drinkers, and the bowl soon gets dirty. Most dogs, some breeds more than others,

◆ **RIGHT**
Puppies hate to be left alone until they are confident that you will quickly return.

SAFETY GUIDELINES ON TOYS FOR DOGS

The jaws and teeth of nearly all dogs are much stronger than you think, so toys should be very tough.

Fluffy dolls will be torn to pieces without fail, so if you must provide them, make sure that they do not have parts that can be detached and swallowed.

Balls are popular toys for dogs because the owners can throw them and join in the game. Fine, but make sure the ball is large enough not even to be half-swallowed by the dog. A dog being rushed to the veterinary surgeon choking on a tennis ball that is stuck in its throat is a common emergency.

The use of a bone as a toy is controversial. Most veterinary surgeons advise against it, unless the bone is so big that the dog cannot break pieces off and swallow them. There is no doubt that a good chew at a bone is a dog's delight.

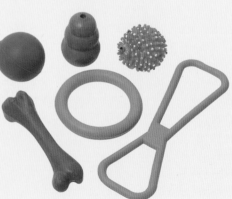

◆ **ABOVE**
Toys should be solid enough not to risk pieces being chewed off and swallowed.

+ LEFT
Hygiene is important for feed bowls. Never add another meal without first thoroughly cleaning the bowl.

are also very splashy drinkers, spilling more water around the bowl than they swallow. So choose your water-bowl site carefully.

The ideal water bowl may be made of ceramic or non-rust metal, but it must be non-spill, and preferably too heavy for the dog to pick up and carry around. If you start with a heavy bowl, the puppy will soon get the idea that this is not a toy to be picked up and carted around, and he will look for something else to play with.

Feed bowls may be much the same as water bowls, with the same idea: the dog should not regard the bowl as a toy. Apart from anything else, if the bowl gets carried around, you can never find it when you want to feed the dog!

The new dog's bed is very important – the bed is the dog's own special place. It is important to introduce the dog to his bed as soon as he arrives, and to insist that the bed is where he sleeps. This may be difficult, but if you give in and let him sleep on your

+ BELOW
Puppies take great comfort from a hot-water bottle, but beware leaks from chewing. An alarm clock seems to soothe them at night.

bed "just until he settles in", you have lost the battle – and probably the war!

To make sure the dog uses his bed, the best way is to shut him into a "bedroom" on the first night with nothing else to choose for a comfortable sleep but the bed. Make sure it is sited away from any draughts. Young puppies will miss their litter mates and perhaps their dam. A useful tip, if the puppy doesn't settle – that's if he is crying pitifully just as you are getting to sleep – is to provide him with

+ BELOW
Rawhide chews are usually an excellent substitute for bones.

comforters. Traditionally, these are a hot-water bottle and a ticking alarm clock; and like many traditions, they often work well.

Toys are important, whatever the age of the dog, but particularly for a young puppy. There is an enormous range on sale, from fluffy dolls that amuse the owner but soon become unrecognizable once the puppy has had a chance to tear them apart, to specifically designed training aids.

Some dogs are obsessive about a particular toy – this occurs more in the terrier breeds than in other types – but mostly dogs have a rather short attention span, dropping one object for another after a short spell of play. There is no certain winner. Each dog has a different fancy, but do provide choice for a puppy, bearing in mind safety guidelines.

BEDS AND BEDDING

The dog must have a bed of his own. From the owner's point of view, washability is the priority. Plastic beds made for this purpose are not expensive and easily cleaned, but they must have soft bedding for comfort.

Providing a mobile cage as a bed and a private place for your puppy has several advantages, not least of which is that there is somewhere to put the puppy when non-doggy friends, who may not appreciate dog hairs all over their clothes, arrive.

Cages may be the completely collapsible type, useful for folding and taking with you when you are travelling with the dog, or, probably better in the long run, the "sky kennel" type which is fastened by nuts and bolts around the middle. This enables the cage to be divided in half for travelling but provides a more permanent kennel for the dog to use at home.

There are plenty of choices of bedding. The most satisfactory from the hygiene point of view, as well as for comfort and warmth, is veterinary bedding, sold under a number of brand names, made of synthetic fur backed by a strong woven base. These veterinary beds may be machine washed, they stay dry as moisture goes straight through them, they are long-lasting, and they are resistant (but not if the dog is really determined!) to being chewed up. They can be bought or cut to any size, and using the principle of "one on, one in the wash", you can easily keep the bed clean and free from doggy odours.

◆ LEFT
Traditional wicker baskets look good until the dog starts to chew the edges. They are not easy to keep clean.

◆ LEFT
Flexible dog beds seem to pass the comfort test. They are usually insulated against cold floors and are easily cleaned. They may be expensive and destructible by determined dogs.

◆ ABOVE, LEFT TO RIGHT
An old blanket is best in a bed rather than just on the floor; synthetic veterinary bedding is probably more hygienic than any other soft bedding; the bean bag is supremely comfortable and warmly insulating; a plastic basket is easily cleaned, but it does need a comfortable lining to be given the dog's personal accolade.

◆ LEFT
Dogs all appreciate a warm covering to lie on, wherever they choose to sleep.

◆ RIGHT
Dogs are thought to be colour-blind –
even though they may choose the
perfect background on which to pose!

BEHAVIOUR TIP

Dogs will often accept your rage
if it means you are paying attention
to them rather than ignoring them.
To ignore your dog is the most
severe punishment you can inflict
on him. So for peaceful nights
for you and your dog, make him
sleep elsewhere.

◆ TOP
The collapsible travelling cage has many uses at
home as well as away.

◆ ABOVE
An outside kennel must be dry, warm and of an
adequate size for the dog's comfort.

◆ RIGHT
An outside kennel and run must always be kept
clean (with wood this may not be easy). The run
is no substitute for proper exercise.

Cushions filled with polystyrene
granules are possibly the most
comfortable of all for the dog, but
they are less easy to wash than
veterinary bedding. Some dogs enjoy
chewing their bed and this results in a
myriad little polystyrene balls rolling
around the floor, which are almost
impossible to sweep up.

Still probably more used than
anything else is a square of old
blanket or a blanket off-cut. Nothing
wrong with them, provided you have
enough so that you can wash them
regularly, bearing in mind that they
leave a fluffy deposit which needs to
be removed from the washing machine
and they take forever to dry.

WHERE TO SLEEP?
The kitchen or a warm utility room are
the best places for the dog to sleep.
The kitchen floor often has non-
absorbent flooring, useful for a puppy

before he's able to avoid accidents.
Once he has become accustomed to
the kitchen, if it remains convenient
to you, it is possibly the best place for
him to stay. The kitchen tends to be
one of the warm places in the house,
and dogs like warmth.

Most dogs are not kennelled out of
doors. There is no particular reason
why they should not be, and if that is
your intention it must be instituted
from the start. Use plenty of warm
bedding and pay attention to draughts
and waterproofing. One problem with
outside kennels is that it becomes too
easy to ignore the dog. Few owners
would indulge in the outright cruelty
of neglecting to feed their dog, but if
the weather doesn't look too good,
plenty would put the walk off to
another day.

If a dog is to be confined in a
kennel, you must ask yourself if you
really want a dog. At worst, the kennel
must provide an adequate exercise
area, as well as the essentials
mentioned above.

HOME, GARDEN AND CAR SAFETY

◆ BELOW
The easiest way for a dog to get out of the garden is via the gate. The gate must be rigid and placed over a hard standing.

Of immediate interest to most new dog owners is the need to make the home and garden dog-proof. This may prove to be a difficult and very expensive undertaking.

You have a responsibility in law to keep your dog under control. This means that your garden must be fenced in such a way as to prevent the dog escaping. As the puppies of almost any breed other than the very smallest grow, so does their ability to jump over fences. There can be no hard and fast rule for the height needed to prevent this; even within the same breed, one will be a jumper and another never learn the skill. However, the minimum height for any dog-proof fence for anything but toy breeds will be 1m (3ft). Often, for dogs from the smaller terrier breeds, like Jack Russells, and the more agile larger breeds, this will not be sufficient. Plenty of dogs can scale a 2m (6ft 6in) fence. A fence this high starts to make the garden look like Fort Knox, and the usual compromise is a fence of about 1.5m (5ft). If it is a wire fence, it must be tightly strung. Many gardens are close fenced to this height, and close fencing has advantages as a dog fence. Being unable to see the world outside often removes the temptation to investigate it.

There are two ways through a fence, even if it is in good repair.

One way is over the top, and the other is underneath. Dogs enjoy digging. You need to be sure that there is no way under. Wire fencing is particularly vulnerable to the tunnelling dog, unless it is firmly attached to some sort of hard, impenetrable base.

Preventing the dog from escaping from the house is usually a matter of care rather than built-in precautions. The perfectly trained dog will not push past his owner when the front door is opened unless required to do so; plenty of others in real life try to. The family has to learn to keep the dog shut in the kitchen when they answer the door – one reason for not restraining the dog's barking when

◆ LEFT
The same device can often be used for children and puppies.

◆ RIGHT
The interior of a car with closed windows may easily reach 130°F (55°C) on a hot day. Install window grills.

◆ BELOW
Electric flexes are dangerous if they are chewed.

someone knocks at the front door; at least the dog is reminding you to shut him away. Downstairs windows, and occasionally upstairs windows, may attract the dog. It is a matter of vigilance unless you are prepared to barricade yourself in.

DOGS IN CARS

The idea of travelling with a dog in the car is very appealing. In the event, it sometimes becomes a nightmare. Part of the very earliest training for the puppy must be to learn to travel in a safe and socially acceptable way in the car. For the smaller breeds, a collapsible cage is ideal.

If your car is a hatchback, a dog guard is an obvious and sensible investment. It needs to be well fitting and strong enough to prevent a determined dog from climbing through it into the front of the car. There are dozens of dog guards

◆ ABOVE AND RIGHT
Dogs may escape despite precautions. Identity discs for collars should have a contact telephone number rather than names and addresses.

designed specifically for each make and model of car. They are advertised in the dog magazines or available from most of the larger dog shows.

Unrestrained dogs in cars cause accidents. If you are not able to use a dog guard or cage, the puppy must be taught to sit on the back seat and never to climb into the front. He will soon learn if you gently and patiently restrain him, and scold him firmly if he comes forward. It is one piece of training where the immediate "no" can work, but not if you sometimes relent and let him sit on the front seat. Harnesses, designed to clip to the rear seat belt fastening, are another way to keep the dog on the back seat.

Some dogs become "barkers" when in the car. This is dangerous and distracting, and steps to remedy it must be taken before the behaviour becomes totally engrained. Specialist advice may be necessary, but the first step is to restrain the dog, with a short lead, below the window level of the car. It's no good shouting at him to shut him up – the dog's response will be to redouble his efforts to be heard above his owner's voice.

BEHAVIOUR TIP

Any response to unacceptable behaviour may be taken by the dog as encouragement. The only sensible response is not to take any obvious notice.

Nutrition and Feeding

The diets of yesteryear, of home-mixed meat and biscuits, have long gone.
Nowadays, professional nutritionists produce feeds of a variety and quality
that should satisfy any dog in forms convenient enough to suit any owner.
Nutrition is a complex subject and there is a simple question: do you know
more about the nutrition of the dog than the experts? Teams of nutritionists
form part of a multi-million pound industry involving science, marketing
and, most importantly, competition between feed companies.
For modern dogs, palatability is considered to be of great importance,
and the professional feed laboratories spend a great deal of time getting
the flavour just right.

◆ FACING PAGE
**It is important to
provide your dog with a
nutritious diet.**

TYPES OF FOOD

Dogs are carnivores. Their digestive system, from the mouth through their intestines, is designed to cope with a meat diet. The dog's teeth are adapted to tear food into swallowable-sized chunks rather than to grind the food, and their stomachs can digest food in this state.

Dogs have probably evolved from animals that lived on a diet of other animals. However, as with the fox in modern times, meat was not always available to them, and the dog is able also to digest and survive on a diet that is mostly vegetable; but a complete absence of meat is likely to lead to nutritional deficiencies.

Foods, whether for dogs or humans, have to supply energy, from which, as well as being the means of movement, the animal's body derives heat, materials for growth and repair, and substances that support these activities. For dogs, this involves a satisfactory mixture of the major nutrients – carbohydrates, fats and proteins – in proportions similar to those required for a healthy human diet; they must also have a sufficient intake of the minor nutrients – vitamins and minerals – in proportions that do differ significantly from the needs of humans.

Dog foods may be divided into several broad categories. For many years the so-called **moist diets** held the major part of the market. They are the tinned foods seen on every supermarket shelf.

Over the past few years other types of food have infiltrated the market. **Complete dry feeds** are becoming increasingly popular. They need minimal preparation – if so desired, they can simply be poured into a dog bowl and given to the dog. Only very slightly more demanding is to pour hot water on to moisten the feed.

Semi-moist diets are not intended to provide a balanced diet on their own. They hold a small but significant place in the market, largely, in all probability, because they involve some degree of preparation before feeding. It is still fairly minimal, involving the addition of carbohydrate supplements as a mixer, often some form of biscuit, to balance the nutritional quality of the food. This is a psychologically important exercise for the owner, who likes to think that he or she is doing something for the dog, as previous generations did when they mixed a bowl of table scraps with some meat and gravy. The one thing to remember is that too much mixing of modern foods can result in nutritional problems. What too often happens is that the concerned owner adds, not just a carbohydrate mixer, but high-protein feed as well, resulting in a diet that is unbalanced, with too much

♦ BELOW
If a dog is hungry and healthy, he will eat. If he is healthy but won't eat, he isn't hungry, so take the food away and let him miss a meal.

NUTRIENTS

The **major nutrients**, required in substantial quantities by every animal, include:

Carbohydrates, which provide the body with energy, and in surplus, will be converted into body fat.

Fats, which are the most concentrated form of energy, producing more than twice as much energy, weight for weight, than carbohydrates, and which will also convert to body fats if supplied in excess.

Proteins, which essentially provide the body-building elements in the diet.

The **minor nutrients** include the vitamins, minerals and trace elements, which, although critical to the animal's health, are required in comparatively small amounts. The vitamins are usually divided into two groups:

Fat soluble: vitamins A, D, E and K.

Water soluble: the B complex vitamins and vitamin C.

◆ BELOW
Each dog should have his own bowl, although the food is often more interesting on the other dog's plate.

◆ ABOVE
Heavy feed bowls make eating easier as they don't skid all over the floor.

protein. There is usually no harm; animals, like man, can deal with an astonishing variety of diet, but too high levels of protein can occasionally exacerbate an existing metabolic problem. There is an old adage: "When all else fails, follow the instructions." It is worth bearing in mind when feeding your dog.

One feature of all modern compound dog foods is that they will contain adequate minor nutrients, which did not always happen in the meat and biscuit days. The outcome is that there is rarely any need for the proprietary feed supplements that are still widely advertised. Calcium, for instance, may have been lacking in some traditional diets, and a bonemeal supplement often used to be recommended. Such a supplement may today do harm in certain circumstances, such as pregnancy in the bitch.

Special diets are a development of the last ten or fifteen years. They are of two types: those that target healthy dogs with special requirements – puppies, for instance, with special growth needs, especially active dogs, and older dogs – and those designed as supportive diets for various illnesses. There are kidney diets, for instance, which control the amount and type of protein the dog is given. These latter special diets are dispensed strictly under the control of a veterinary surgeon, many of whom are now trained specifically in the use of such diets.

◆ LEFT
Canned food must be used within twenty-four hours of opening and kept refrigerated. Cover open cans with plastic lids, and reserve an opener and fork just for dog food.

◆ LEFT
Dogs love bones but vets don't because of the risks of bowel stoppages or choking. Very large bones minimize such risk. Never give a dog a chop bone.

FOOD REQUIREMENTS

Dogs are adaptable creatures. They can, for instance, utilize protein foods, like meats, for energy if their intake of carbohydrates is deficient. They must, however, be provided with a minimum level of each of around thirty nutrients, including the vitamins and minerals, if they are to stay healthy. All the modern prepared foods, and the great majority of home-mixed diets, will provide an adequate supply of essential nutrients.

Some animal protein is essential to maintain a dog's health. A vegetarian diet for dogs can be devised but requires skill, although there is no doubt that dogs do not need the level of animal protein in their diet that is commonly provided.

Some fats are also vital in the diet, providing certain essential fatty acids, and acting as carriers for the fat-soluble vitamins.

Carbohydrates form the bulk of most diets, including normal dog foods, whether commercially compounded or home-mixed.

Provided your dog's diet has a reasonable balance of the major nutrients, and the foods are not themselves wildly out of the ordinary, the owner's concern need only be with the actual quantity given to the dog, and the total calorie provision.

Butcher's scraps, canned or fresh, is not a complete feed.

Canned chicken must be balanced with other foods.

Frozen chicken is an inexpensive way of providing meat protein for small dogs.

Commercial canned food may be a complete feed or mixed.

Rice is a source of carbohydrates for home mixing.

Dry complete feeds have become very popular.

Semi-moist feeds must be kept in sealed packets.

The traditional feed of biscuits with gravy.

Dog biscuits are not adequate as a dog's only food.

At first sight the figures in the table below suggest that the obvious, and cheapest, way to feed a dog is to give it biscuits alone. They offer the highest calorie content, weight for weight, of any food except pure fat, and dog biscuits are cheaper to buy than canned foods. But this is misleading because a diet that consisted solely of dog biscuits would be seriously deficient in protein, and it would be deficient in fats, vitamins and minerals.

AVERAGE CALORIE REQUIREMENTS FOR 24 HOURS

Growing puppies:	6 weeks	3 months	6 months
Terriers, mature weight 10kg (22lb)	330	530	700
German Shepherds, mature weight 30kg (66lb)	1200	1800	2600
Giant breeds, mature weight 50kg (110lb)	1950	2500	4000
Adult dogs:	maintenance:		
Terriers	400		
German Shepherds	1600		
Giant breeds	2400		

The table gives average amounts and should be regarded as a guide only. Take account of whether the mature dog on this level of food intake is gaining or losing weight. Puppies should gain weight steadily, without becoming too fat.

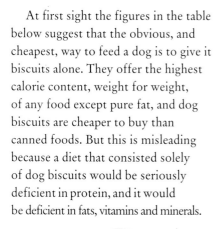

Meaty treats make excellent rewards.

Most dogs enjoy bone-shaped biscuits, and hard-baked (so safer) bones.

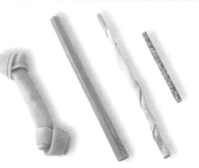

Chews made out of raw or processed hide are usually a safe substitute for bones.

Give only special formula dog drops (see panel below for warnings about human chocolate).

Some biscuits include a charcoal variety, intended to help digestive problems.

Biscuit treats are produced in various flavours.

CHOCOLATE AND CANINES

Experts agree that certain chemicals in chocolate can be toxic to dogs, especially in large quantities. The chemical theobromine, found especially in dark (bittersweet) and baker's chocolate, can cause a toxic reaction, while caffeine may also lead to digestive problems. Reactions will vary according to dog weight and sensitivity, and although most owners report few or no ill effects where only small amounts have been consumed, it is safest to avoid giving your dog any chocolate.

CALORIE CONTENT OF COMMON FOOD PER 100G (3½OZ)

Dog biscuits used as mixer feeds	300–360
Fresh meat	140
Soft, moist, complete feeds	320
Dry complete feeds	270

MANUFACTURER'S DECLARED CALORIE CONTENT PER 100G (3½OZ) IN THEIR RANGE OF CANNED FOODS (HILL'S SCIENCE DIET)

Canine Growth	136
Canine Maintenance	126
Canine Performance	140
Canine Maintenance Light	87
Canine Senior	117

Regular veterinary
examination of older
dogs will reveal the
possible existence
of nutritionally
controllable diseases.

SPECIAL DIETS

Quality of feed is particularly
important during puppyhood, to
provide nutrients for the rapidly
growing animal. Similarly, an in-whelp
bitch needs high-quality food if she is
to produce healthy puppies without
putting undue strain on her own
bodily resources. Pregnant animals
will deplete their own tissues to
provide sufficient nutrients for their
puppies both in the uterus and
afterwards when they are suckling. A
bitch with a litter of several puppies
will almost inevitably lose some
weight; her condition needs to be
watched carefully. There is no point,
however, in over-feeding the bitch
while she is pregnant.

There may be specific demands for
particularly active adult dogs, for the
older dog, and for the overweight dog.
Scientifically formulated diets are
designed to provide for these various
special requirements.

Several pet food manufacturers
provide prescription diets that, used
under veterinary supervision, aid in
the management of a number of
diseases. They are only obtainable
through a veterinary surgeon.

The range is wide and includes
products that may either contain
greater proportions of certain
nutrients than usual – one is a high-
fibre diet, for instance, which may be
of benefit in cases of diabetes, and in
fibre responsive intestinal problems –
or smaller elements of the normal diet.
Low-protein diets assist in the control
of chronic kidney disease, low-sodium
diets are used in the management of
congestive heart failure.

◆ ABOVE
If puppies share a
bowl of food it is
difficult to be sure
they both get a
fair share.

DAILY CALORIE REQUIREMENT FOR THE OVERWEIGHT DOG

Target weight	Scale 1	Scale 2
2.5kg (5½lb)	120	90
5kg (11lb)	200	160
7kg (15½lb)	275	220
10kg (22lb)	350	270
12kg (26½lb)	400	320
15kg (33lb)	470	375
20kg (44lb)	600	470
25kg (55lb)	700	550
30kg (66lb)	800	650
40kg (88lb)	1000	800

OBESITY

One of the commonest afflictions in the dog is simple obesity. Owners will frequently not see it and, once acknowledged, it may still be extremely difficult for them to understand that reducing the dog's food intake is not cruel. The obesity diet has its part to play by enabling the owner to feed a low-calorie diet to the dog, which will satisfy the hunger pangs while reducing his intake of nutrients.

This table indicates a suitable intake of calories for an overweight dog with a target weight indicated in the first column. The diet needs to be balanced by sensible variations of other nutrients.

You can see from this just how few calories, and consequently how little food, a dog really needs if he is to lose weight at a satisfactory rate. Scale 1 will cause reduction in body weight at a fairly slow rate, and even with ordinary foodstuffs the dog should not be too drastically hungry. Scale 2 is necessary when a more rapid reduction in weight is called for. It is still not a drastic diet regime.

As an example, if you wished to reduce your dog's weight to 20kg (44lb), using the slower scale you would need to feed not more than 600 calories a day. Without resorting to a special diet, this could be achieved by a total daily feed of 115g (about 4oz) of meat and 130g (4½oz) of biscuit mixer. This is not a lot of food on a large dog's plate, and it explains why special reducing diets, which give bulk and fill the dog's stomach, are popular.

♦ RIGHT
Obesity is best controlled by careful attention to diet before the dog's weight gets out of hand.

Grooming

Grooming your dog performs two functions. The obvious one is to keep him looking, and smelling, acceptable to you and to other people. The second one is just as important. Grooming, of a very different sort, between dogs establishes and maintains the relative status of each dog. By daily grooming you are telling the dog, in the most gentle terms, that you are in charge. The whole ritual of insisting that your dog stands while you brush and comb him emphasizes that when push comes to shove, what you say goes. There is no more important lesson in dog training.

◆ FACING PAGE
Grooming should
be an enjoyable
interaction between
dog and owner.

EQUIPMENT AND HOME GROOMING

Many owners of long-coated breeds positively enjoy grooming their dogs, often achieving and maintaining near professional results. It demands a great deal of dedication, and time – the show trim of a poodle, for instance, is the result of several days hard work in total, possibly spread over a week or more. Owners of short-coated breeds are likely to be less dedicated to such perfection, although regular grooming is still necessary to maintain the dog's skin and coat in good condition.

Whatever the intention, you will need the proper equipment. For trimmed breeds, clippers are essential. Electric clippers are probably the most expensive item of actual grooming equipment, although grooming stands or tables can cost any price, depending on their construction and how firmly you feel it is necessary to restrain the

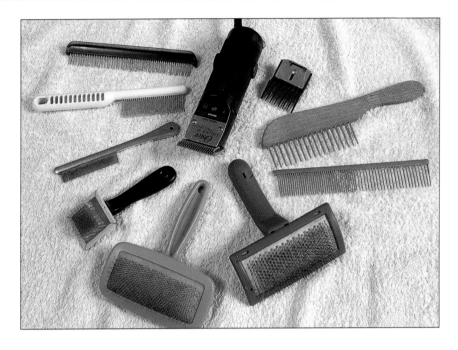

◆ BELOW
Professional grooming is a considerable skill and demands a detailed knowledge of every breed on which work is undertaken.

dog. Professional clippers do the best job and last longest, but a compromise on price and effectiveness can usually be reached. Whatever the make or cost of the clippers, they must be regularly sharpened. This is a job for the expert, and there are several companies in every country that specialize in a prompt and inexpensive service. Do not be tempted to economize. The dog won't like it, and you won't be happy with the result.

Most breeders of long-coated dogs do their own grooming. They will be happy to advise on the equipment that is suitable for your level of skill, and they usually will help the novice to get started. But don't expect show-winning results immediately, even with the best tools.

In addition to clippers, you will need a suitable brush and comb. There are many types. Again, take advice from breeders. The hard brush that is suitable for a mixture of massage and loose hair removal for a Boxer, say, may be death to the silky coat of an Afghan, and, conversely, a comb will do very little for the short coat of an untrimmed breed.

Many people give up on some of the long-coated breeds. They love the dog, but hate the regular chore of trimming and grooming and the coat-matting that is the inevitable result of failure to do both. Taking the scissors to such dogs is not an option. If you were tempted by a beautifully shaggy dog but find the reality all too overwhelming, there may be no alternative to taking most of the coat off. But please let a professional do it. Both you and the dog will feel less embarrassed at the result.

1 This Shih Tzu takes every bit as long to groom as an Afghan many times its size.

2 The first stage is to gently brush out the knots that always occur.

3 *(right)* Thoroughly brush the dog's entire coat, including the legs and tail.

4 A final grooming brings up the coat.

5 *(right)* The resplendent result – but for how long?

GROOMING FOR DIFFERENT COATS

Short-coated dogs may need less attention than other types and usually require no professional care at all. The downside to owning a short-coated dog is that they moult all the time, sometimes more than others. Dedicated owners of the short-coated breeds, especially breeds with white coats like Bull Terriers, will tell you that there is no colour or type of clothing that you can wear that does not get covered in dog hairs.

Daily grooming helps. A brush with stiff but not harsh bristles is all that is required, and it takes about ten minutes. Be careful to avoid the eyes, but otherwise brush the entire body.

Rough-coated dogs may need more attention. Some rough coats do not moult in the way that short coats do, but they "cast", which is a more substantial moult, every six months or so. When they cast, hair is lost in mats, especially if the dog has not been regularly groomed throughout the rest of the year.

Regular, daily brushing and combing will prevent the coat matting. Again, a stiff brush is the main piece of equipment, but a comb is also useful. It is essential to brush or comb right through the thickness of the coat. Just skimming over the top is of very little use.

Some rough-coated breeds need occasional attention from a professional groomer, particularly if you are intending to try your hand in the show-ring. All those artfully dishevelled creatures you see at major shows are the result of hours of attention by their dedicated owners.

The **silky-coated breeds** – such as Cocker Spaniels and Irish Setters – need exactly the same attention as

SHORT COAT

1 A short-bristled brush is being used to clean the coat of this Brittany.

2 A wire-bristled glove makes easy work for short-haired breeds that need minimal attention.

ROUGH COAT

1 Rough-coated terriers need more attention to their coats than is realized.

2 Regular, daily brushing out is essential. This dog looks about ready for a professional trim.

SILKY COAT

1 Dogs with long, silky coats demand much grooming. The coat should never be clipped.

2 Careful grooming right through the coat with a not-too-stiff brush must be a daily task.

A Standard Poodle in perfect show trim, called the lion trim.

No breed is more difficult to keep in perfect trim than the Old English Sheepdog.

TRIMMING THE POODLE

The Poodle is generally thought of as a trimmed dog, and the prospective owner usually realizes what is likely to be required. Daily attention is still necessary, but the monthly visit to the dog parlour may become a welcome ritual.

The exaggerated trim, derived from a working cut of long ago (the Poodle was originally a gundog), is not essential to these breeds and a version of the puppy trim can be carried on throughout the dog's life. This is simply a closer trim all over without the topiary of the show dog. Many owners feel it still keeps the essential nature of the breed. It takes less grooming than a show trim, but nevertheless needs daily attention. It also still needs regular attention from the professional to keep it in shape. The coats of ungroomed Poodles quickly get into an appalling state.

rough-coated dogs. Some tend to grow rather heavy coats and need to be trimmed regularly.

The breeds that demand really skilled attention are, of course, the **long-coated** ones – Poodles of all sizes, Old English Sheepdogs, the trimmed terriers.

Question one, therefore, is, "do you want the expense and the trouble of professional grooming for your dog every four weeks?" This is the question that many prospective dog owners fail to ask themselves. Sadly, the typical result is the Old English Sheepdog that has its coat trimmed to the skin to keep it socially acceptable. A beautifully groomed dog is seen on television advertisements and the

family all cry, "That is the dog we want." But none of them has the time or the inclination to spend a long time every day, brushing and combing and cleaning up their new dog; and still less when the novelty has worn off.

So if you must have a dog that needs a lot of daily work, be sure you are going to be happy to spend the time on it. Before you make up your mind, go and see the breeder to find out just what is involved.

Expert owners and breeders will usually trim their own dogs, but if you are getting one of the trimmed breeds as a family pet, it is sensible to contact

your local grooming parlour with your puppy as soon as it is allowed out. The groomer will give you advice on daily care of the puppy's coat, and discuss with you when to start trimming, and what you can best do to keep the dog's coat in good shape between professional visits.

The coat of the Afghan is long and very fine-textured. Gentle but thorough grooming is necessary to maintain its condition.

BATHING A DOG

Dog owners in temperate climates are generally reluctant to bathe their dogs, remembering all sorts of old wives' tales regarding the adverse effects of doing so. These are probably the same arguments that people used in the Middle Ages about their own personal hygiene.

Some dogs may not need to be bathed, especially the short-coated breeds that tend to shrug off dirt; but the smell may remain.

There are, in fact, very few breeds of dog in which regular bathing causes any ill effects, although it is sometimes cited by breeders whose dogs' coats are less than ideal for the breed. "The new owner must have over-bathed or over-groomed the puppy" can be a convenient excuse. Some breeds should never, according to the

WHERE TO BATH THE DOG

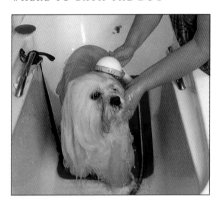

1 Early training makes the task of bathing a dog easier, but few of them actually enjoy it.

2 A double-drainer sink is suitable for small breeds, while the family bath can be pressed into service for larger dogs.

♦ BELOW
Nail clipping is a regular necessity for many dogs. If you are not confident of your skill, ask a professional to do it – if you clip into the quick of the nail you will never be able to persuade the dog to submit to the task again.

breeders, be bathed. These are the dogs that veterinary surgeons can smell through the door when the dog is brought to the surgery!

In many tropical or sub-tropical countries dogs must be bathed weekly, without fail, if certain tick-borne diseases are to be avoided. There is no evidence of poor coats in show dogs in these countries.

There are three types of dog shampoo: the straightforward medicated shampoo, the anti-parasitic shampoo, and specialized, veterinary shampoos, which may be prescribed for particular skin conditions. If a dog is prone to allergies, any of these may precipitate one, but rarely. Shampoos from a reputable source will minimize such problems.

BATHING TIPS

1 A very small dog may fit into a basin, but wear waterproofs for the moment when it tips and spills everywhere.

2 Rubbing the dog semi-dry will prevent some of the water splashing all around the room when he shakes himself – which he will do shortly.

3 A good shake should be followed by some vigorous exercise to complete the drying out process.

4 Avoid getting water into the eyes during bathing, and wipe around them once the dog is out of the bath.

5 Grooming while the coat is still slightly damp, but not wet, will help make the job of removing tangles much easier.

6 *(right)* Clean and sweet smelling until some more horse manure to roll in is found.

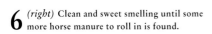

Breeding

There are tens of thousands of four-legged reasons for not breeding from your dog. They occupy hundreds of welfare and rescue kennels. So consider very carefully indeed whether you are at risk of adding to the large number of unwanted dogs. If you decide to go ahead, it is a most rewarding experience. Never decide to breed in the expectation that you will make money. It is almost certainly not true – the appetites of eight unsold twelve-week-old puppies are devastating – and you would be breeding for all the wrong reasons.

✦ FACING PAGE
Breeding from your dog can be very satisfying. However, it does entail a lot of hard work and should not be entered into lightly.

To Breed or Not to Breed

The first thing to consider is that you cannot expect a crossbred dog or bitch to produce puppies in his or her own image. If you own a crossbred, and your reason for breeding is that friends have said that they want one "just like her", remember that the chances of a litter producing even one puppy that is just like its mother are small to very small.

Crossbred dogs, by reason of their own breeding, have a wider genetic pool than purebred animals. Any selection of the characteristics of either parent is a matter of chance, and the greater the variety of characteristics for nature to select from, the greater will be the differences between puppies in the litter, and the greater the difference between the puppies and their parents.

If you breed from parents of mixed ancestry, you will produce puppies that may not even remotely resemble the dog or bitch that your friends were looking for. Potential buyers may well melt away.

◆ LEFT
The standard Schnauzer, the middle size of the Schnauzer breeds, is not very common in English-speaking countries but is a delightful dog.

◆ BELOW LEFT
Looking after a litter of puppies is very demanding work for bitch and owner alike. For both it may easily involve many twenty-four hour days.

But it is not only with crossbred dogs that the phenomenon of the melting buyer exists. Many litters of purebred dogs are bred on the apparent promise that several friends are anxious to have a puppy of that breed, just like yours. From the time of your bitch coming into season there will be about two weeks before she is mated, nine weeks before the litter arrives, and another eight weeks before the puppies are ready to go to their new homes. That's nineteen weeks since the friends made their remarks – over four months for the enthusiasm to wane, for their circumstances to change, or for them to become really keen and buy a puppy from elsewhere. If you think this is a cynical attitude, try asking for a small deposit.

There are, however, good and sensible reasons for breeding.

The dog or bitch should be purebred. One or other should either be of a good working strain – and have shown itself to be a good working dog in the field – or be a sufficiently good show dog for the breeder or an expert to recommend that you should breed from it. The most straightforward way to determine the animal's show quality is to exhibit at shows with success.

The reason for restricting breeding to these two groups of animals is that

To many people the Airedale Terrier is an old-fashioned breed. It is less spoiled than most, but has the typical terrier temperament.

In every healthy litter the puppies are looking for mischief as soon as they are able to run around.

there is much less likelihood of your being left with puppies on your hands, or worse, running the risk of sending them to unsuitable homes. No reputable breeder would ever do this.

Remember that buyers of purebred puppies want the best, which means that both parents have shown their quality.

A litter of puppies is great fun. But after seven or eight weeks the fun may

become an expensive and exhausting chore. Being left with six or more fourteen-week old crossbred puppies that are starting to show that they had Great Dane somewhere in their ancestry is not as amusing as it sounds.

The same applies whether you own the dog or bitch. There may not be the same imperatives if you own the dog and the bitch belongs to the lady down the road, but you both have the same responsibility for the outcome.

There is no truth in the commonly held belief that siring a litter will in any way settle a dog down. Neither is there any truth in the belief that a bitch needs to have a litter. There is no medical reason for either belief. The reverse may very well be true as far as the male is concerned.

The pregnant bitch needs special care and feeding but should continue to exercise regularly until the day she whelps.

Cleanliness in the litter box is, as they say, "next to dogliness".

CHOOSING MATING PARTNERS

THE STUD DOG

Stud dogs are always selected from the best. This may mean nothing more than being currently the most fashionable, but to be among the fashionable always means that the dog has sufficient merit, either as a working dog or as a show dog, to have attracted widespread attention.

It would be unusual for someone's pet dog to become a stud dog, but if a number of fellow enthusiasts ask if they can use your dog, take advice from someone you trust in the breed. Handling matings is a skilled job. If you want to learn, become an apprentice to an expert.

The better, or more fashionable, the stud dog, the higher will be the fee payable for his services. As a guide, the stud fee is likely to be somewhat lower than the price you might expect to get for a puppy. Special arrangements such as "pick of litter" are by no means

◆ BELOW
The Boxer is a very popular breed. There should be no difficulty in finding the dog to suit your bitch.

◆ LEFT
This outstanding Rough Collie may be the ideal stud dog.

uncommon. This means the stud dog owner has the right to pick whichever he or she regards as the best puppy from the litter, either in lieu of the fee, or as a consideration for a reduced fee.

However, it is not necessary or even desirable to go to the most fashionable stud dog for your bitch's mating. An experienced breeder will advise on which dog to choose, using

the physical appearance and pedigree of your bitch and the available dogs as a guide. Some breeders take more notice of pedigree, others of conformation. Learn about the breed, and decide how close to your ideal each breeder's stock is.

PEDIGREES AND CHAMPIONS

The Kennel Club has sole responsibility for registration of pedigree dogs in Great Britain. National clubs have the same responsibility in their own countries throughout the world. The American Kennel Club, although not the only registration authority in the United States, reciprocates its registrations with the Kennel Club and the Federation Cynologique Internationale (FCI), to which the Australian Kennel Control is federated.

Most Kennel Clubs have reciprocal arrangements, and dogs registered in one country can be re-registered in another if the dog is imported. Official pedigrees are derived from the registration particulars of all purebred dogs that are themselves registered with the Kennel Club. Unless a dog is itself registered, its offspring cannot in turn be registered, except in certain special circumstances. Pedigree records are held for at least four generations, although some breeders will be able to show you much longer ones than that.

Different countries have different criteria for awarding the title of Champion. In the United Kingdom the title is awarded to show dogs and working dogs. Some aspire to, and some achieve, both titles.

To become a Champion in the United Kingdom a show dog must have been awarded three Challenge Certificates under different judges,

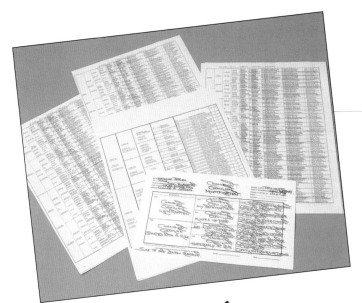

◆ LEFT
Careful noting of pedigree and breeding records is essential if you are serious about your breeding programme.

◆ BELOW
The Cairn Terrier, another popular breed.

◆ RIGHT
All breeding programmes start from small beginnings but may end with a Champion like this Yorkshire Terrier.

with at least one of the certificates being awarded after the dog has reached the age of twelve months. Challenge Certificates are awarded to the best dog and bitch in each breed at specified Championship Shows. The term Challenge Certificate derives from the fact that the judge may invite any or all unbeaten dogs from earlier classes to challenge the winner of the open class for the certificate.

The Australian system is identical to that of the United Kingdom, but in the US Championships are gained under a points system with points awarded in different fields: breed, obedience, field and herding.

The qualifications for Champions in working dogs take account of the dog's success in the working trials.

FINDING HOMES FOR THE PUPPIES

There is no point in breeding from a bitch unless you can expect to sell the puppies. Your best bet is to produce a litter that will be acceptable to enthusiasts, unless you have firm orders that ensure the sale of your puppies. The breeder of your bitch may be able to help. In many breeds, good puppies are at a premium. Reputable breeders will be asked regularly when or where there is a litter due. Your bitch's breeder may be happy to pass on applicants to you, and to explain to them about the breeding of your bitch.

◆ ABOVE
At three weeks old all puppies are delightful, but this pair are likely to get into mischief next week.

◆ LEFT
A rough and tumble is a vital part of the puppies' learning process.

MATING

♦ BOTTOM
Dogs will be interested in the bitch from day one of her season, but she will usually refuse to mate until she is in full oestrus.

THE BREEDING CYCLE

Male dogs become sexually mature at about six months of age. From that time their sexual behaviour is not cyclical, and they are capable of mating at any time and almost any place!

The bitch usually comes into season for the first time when she is aged about nine months, and fairly regularly every six months thereafter. It is not unusual, nor is it in any way abnormal, for the first season to be earlier, even as young as six months, or for it to be postponed until the bitch is over a year old. Neither is it unusual or abnormal for the interval between seasons to be longer than six months. If the interval between one

season and another is very much less than six months, and particularly if it has become irregular in this respect, there may be some abnormality, and advice should be sought from your veterinary surgeon.

A bitch's season lasts for about three weeks. She will show some swelling of her vulva shortly before presenting a blood-stained discharge. The discharge is usually very bloody at the start of her season, becoming paler after about ten days.

Although no risks should be taken from the first signs of season, the bitch will normally not accept a dog until about halfway through the season, at which time she will become

fertile (i.e. capable of conceiving). There is normally no odour detectable to a human from a bitch in season, but there is a very powerful one detectable by dogs a considerable distance away. Do not assume that because you live a mile from the nearest male dog, your bitch will not be mated.

Do not assume, either, that a dog that lives together with a bitch, though they may be brother and sister, will not be interested.

MATING AND CONCEPTION

True oestrus begins at about twelve days from the first signs of the bitch coming into season. From that time she will accept the male's attempts to

◆ BELOW
Mating takes place when the bitch has ovulated. Ejaculation occurs quickly, and the tie is not necessary for conception.

◆ BELOW
Although not essential, the tie has a physiological function in helping the sperm to move up the genital tract.

mate her, and will be fertile, for about five to seven days. Ovulation, the release of eggs into the uterus, takes place during this period. The timing is variable, and the dog and bitch are the best practical arbiters of the bitch's fertile period, although laboratory tests are available to help timing if the bitch fails to conceive.

The mating act may be prolonged. Once the dog has ejaculated, the bitch continues to grip his penis in her vagina, by means of a ring muscle, for up to about twenty minutes. The dog may climb off the bitch's back, and turn to face the other way, but both stand "tied". The tie is not actually essential for a successful mating, although all breeders prefer to see it.

Pregnancy lasts for about sixty-three days from mating. The normal variation is from about sixty days to as much as sixty-seven. Outside this range veterinary attention should be sought, although it does not necessarily indicate a problem and may simply be an extension of normal variation.

Bitches should not be bred from until they are physically mature. The ideal age for a first litter is about two years old.

◆ LEFT
Bitches should continue with normal exercise throughout pregnancy, although they are likely to become increasingly placid for its duration.

◆ BELOW
The bitch should be introduced to her whelping box at least a week before whelping is due in order to give her time to become comfortable with her surroundings.

WHELPING

Whelping is a natural event. In nine cases out of ten there is no need for human interference; in ninety-nine cases out of a hundred, interference takes place before it is necessary.

Be prepared. Let your veterinary surgeon know well in advance. He or she may have confirmed that the bitch is in whelp, but ask the vet to note the expected date on the calendar.

Make sure that you have decided where the bitch is to whelp, and that

breeders will show you a suitable box with a rail around the edge to prevent the bitch lying on her puppies and squashing them. Some bitches are very clumsy. Bedding for the box needs to be disposable – whelpings are accompanied by a great deal of mess. Almost universally the basic bedding for a whelping box is newspaper in large quantities, so start saving them some weeks in advance. You can always do the crossword

while you are waiting for the puppies to arrive!

Most bitches give warning of imminent whelping by going off their food. If you have a thermometer you may use it at this stage. A dog's normal temperature is approximately 101.5°F (38.5°C). A drop in temperature of two or three degrees nearly always indicates that the bitch will start to whelp within twenty-four hours. For several days before whelping, many

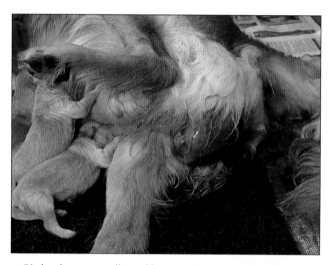

1 Bitches do not normally need human assistance to produce their puppies, although whelping may be a prolonged business.

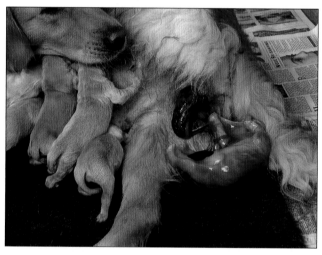

2 The bitch breaks the puppy out of the foetal membranes and often eats the membranes. It is not usually necessary to tie off the cord.

she has agreed with you. If it is to be in a special place, and in a special bed, introduce her to it a week or two in advance, and teach her that it is now her bed. The ideal place is a quiet corner without passing traffic, and away from where the children play. Bear in mind that you, or the vet, may have to attend to her at some stage. Under the stairs may not be perfect for this reason.

She should have a whelping box. It needs to be large to accommodate the bitch and a litter, which may number as many as twelve puppies. Most

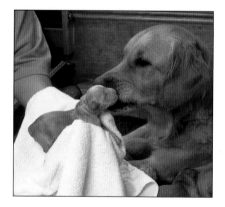

3 The puppy needs plenty of stimulation by licking from the bitch or, if necessary, by rubbing in a towel, to be sure that it is breathing satisfactorily.

bitches will start to make a nest somewhere, usually somewhere inappropriate. Most bitches become very restless a few hours before they start to whelp.

Right up to the point of producing her first puppy, a family pet that in the nature of things is used to human company will probably want the comfort of human attention, but once she starts to strain for the first puppy, the great majority of bitches will become uninterested in the people around them and just get on with the job of producing a litter.

◆ BELOW
New-born puppies spend virtually all their time
drinking or sleeping. If the litter is restless,
urgent attention should be sought.

◆ BELOW RIGHT
With a large litter it would be wise to make
sure all the puppies get their share.

It may take several hours from the time the bitch starts to strain until the first puppy is delivered. Provided she is continuing to strain, there is no panic. If, after serious effort for an hour or more, she stops trying, ask your veterinary surgeon for advice.

The first sign that a puppy is due is the appearance of the water bag. This is an apt description for the foetal membranes; they look just like a small bag of water, which appears through the vagina. Do not attempt to remove it; it has the function of enlarging the birth canal to permit the following puppy to pass through.

The puppy may be born either head or tail first. Each is as common as the other, and the appearance of the tail first does not indicate a breach birth.

The first puppy may take some time to be born after you get first sight of it, and it may often seem to disappear back up the canal. The time for concern is when the puppy is obviously stuck fast with no movement up or down, despite continued straining, or when the bitch appears to have given up straining and is lying exhausted. Veterinary attention is needed urgently.

CAESARIAN OPERATIONS
Veterinary assistance at a whelping is as likely to involve a caesarian operation as not. The bitch is too small to allow very much manipulation if she has problems producing puppies. In earlier times assisted whelping involved the use of instruments inserted into her vagina, but this has largely been discontinued in favour of surgery. Caesarians are now more popular, partly for humane reasons, but mainly because of the

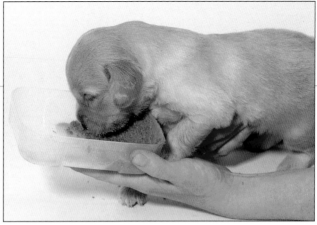

◆ LEFT
Puppies are able to
eat solid food from
about two weeks on.

◆ BELOW
Any puppies that do
not get their share
may be bottle fed
successfully with a
suitable bitch-milk
substitute.

existence of low-risk anaesthetics coupled with surgical techniques that have improved so much over the years that a successful outcome of the operation can usually be anticipated.

To produce live puppies and a healthily recovering bitch, the operation must be carried out earlier rather than later. The subject should be discussed with the veterinary surgeon well before the whelping is due, so that both parties know the other's feeling about the operation. The veterinary surgeon must be called in before the bitch has become exhausted from straining unsuccessfully to produce her puppies.

Sadly, some breeds have such a poor reputation for natural whelping that caesarian operations are carried out routinely, without waiting for indications of failure by the bitch. Breeders in these breeds must reconsider their whole outlook on dog breeding if their breeds are to continue to be popular.

Other than in these special circumstances, caesarian operations are usually carried out as a matter of emergency. Most veterinary surgeons will ask you to bring the bitch to the surgery if there are whelping difficulties, rather than visit the house, so that operating facilities are at hand.

The otherwise healthy bitch and her puppies will thrive best back in her home environment, and the veterinary surgeon will release them as soon as possible. Once home she may need a little coaxing to accept and feed the puppies; as far as she is concerned, they just appeared while she was asleep. Careful introductions almost always work, but she may need some help initially to attach the puppies to the teats. Once they are sucking

normally, the bitch will realize what she is supposed to do.

After the first day or two, a bitch who has had a caesarian may be treated the same as a bitch who has produced the puppies naturally.

AFTER WHELPING

The puppies must be cleaned behind every time they feed. This stimulates the passage of urine and faeces; without the stimulation they will not pass excreta and may become fatally constipated. This is one of the bitch's jobs. If she has been under anaesthetic, she may not realize this. Holding the puppy tail first to her will quickly teach her the routine.

Normally, the bitch remains with her puppies constantly for at least the first couple of weeks. There may be difficulty in persuading her to leave them even for her own natural functions. If this is the case, don't worry. She will go eventually. Let her do it in her own time.

A healthy bitch with puppies quickly develops a large appetite. For the first few days it may be necessary to feed her in or very close to her bed, but make sure there is plenty of food available, and particularly plenty of fluids. She may prefer milk. Forget the once a day feeding routine; let her have food whenever she wants it. She has an enormous task.

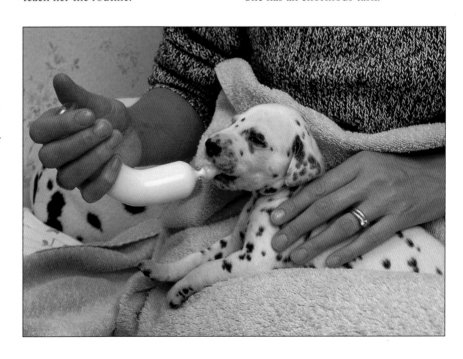

REARING
PUPPIES

The first two weeks are the easiest.
The puppies are relatively inert. They
will wriggle around the bed a great
deal but are incapable of recovering
the nest if they accidentally fall out.
Most whelping boxes have high fronts
for this reason.

At this stage the puppies need no
supplementary feeding, just their
dam's milk, and should spend most
of their time sleeping quietly. If they
do not, seek help urgently.

Puppies open their eyes at about
ten days old, though some breeds are
notoriously lazy about this.

◆ RIGHT
Five-week-old puppies are active and
alert and already learning lessons
about the world.

By about three weeks old the
puppies are moving around much
more; they will mostly have fallen out
of the box several times, indicating
that it is time to add another layer to
the barrier at the front. It may also be
the time to start to supplement their
diet. This is done by hand-feeding.

Although most people think of
the puppies' first hand-feeding as an
occasion for something delicate, milky
perhaps, just try scraping a little raw
beef from the joint on to your fingers.
You will be lucky to have a finger left!

The main reason for starting to wean
puppies at three weeks is to spare the

◆ ABOVE
At three days old the puppy's eyes are still
closed, and its only active movement is likely
to be towards its dam for feeding.

◆ ABOVE
By three weeks old the puppy will be trying
to get out of the nest box.

◆ BELOW
By eight weeks it is time for the puppies to
leave home, usually to the relief of their dam
and often to the relief of their owner.

bitch. With a large litter there is a
tremendous physical demand on her,
and she will certainly lose a lot of
weight during the course of rearing a
litter. By starting to wean the puppies
relatively early she will be spared some
of this load. Puppies do, in any case,
start to look for more solid food at
this age if given the opportunity.

At three weeks of age the litter
must have its first worming dose.
Take advice on this. Modern wormers
cause no side effects.

From three weeks to about five
weeks a gradually increasing
proportion of the puppies' diet should
be supplied from sources other than
their dam. By six weeks they should be
completely weaned, although the dam
may take some convincing of this,
and may keep trying to feed the pups.
The action of sucking by the puppies
prolongs the production of milk by
the dam, and after six weeks this
should be discouraged.

At six weeks the puppies should
be feeding on a puppy food of your
choice. It is also time for a second
worming dose to be given.

Training

Every dog is capable of learning a great deal more than is generally recognized. Although it may take a special type of dog and a special type of owner to create a canine film star, home helper or agility champion, there is no reason why every dog should not achieve the essential basics of obedience and well-socialized behaviour. A well-trained dog is less likely to develop unwanted behaviour patterns, partly because dogs often adopt bad habits when they are bored. Dogs enjoy the stimulation of training and most love to please their owners too.

◆ FACING PAGE
There are many ways that a trained dog is capable of helping its owner.

SOCIALIZING YOUR PUPPY

All puppies need to meet as many other dogs and as many people as possible. This is the essence of socialization, and when done effectively most of the behaviour problems that may occur later will be avoided.

From the day you acquire him, your new puppy should start to meet other people. The puppy must not be overwhelmed but, within reason, the more people he meets the better. The visitors should be asked to hold the puppy, handling and cuddling him gently, so that he learns that people are friends. However, until the puppy has had his vaccinations some caution is necessary to avoid second-hand contact with other owners' dogs. Ask dog owners to delay their visit until your puppy has had his second round of injections.

Apart from other dogs in the household, to which the puppy should be introduced at the earliest possible moment, meeting dogs must be delayed until the new puppy has had his two sets of injections and the "all clear" from the veterinary surgeon, at about twelve weeks old.

In the United Kingdom, one of the most useful, as well as entertaining, developments in puppy training in recent years has been the creation of puppy parties. These are exactly what they sound like. Once or twice a week a group of puppy owners with their puppies meet for an hour or so in the village hall or somewhere similar. Puppies from twelve weeks of age up to six or seven months, and of all sizes, are allowed to play with each other with only the minimum restraint from their owners. The smaller ones are rarely overwhelmed by the larger, and all learn that their fellow canines can be approached without fear. It is an object lesson for their owners.

The puppy party has revolutionized dog training in the United Kingdom. Most puppy groups have experienced trainers in charge, and the transition from pure play into early obedience training can be seamless. Lead training is nearly always part of it, perhaps simply walking at heel without tugging, and the foundations to more advanced work may be laid.

Puppy playgroups introduce all shapes and sizes of dogs to each other and help to overcome alarm at strange animals.

Basic training classes are held in village halls, or similar places, all over the world. Attendance at a weekly class is usually sufficient.

EARLY LEARNING

Teaching the dog good habits is best achieved by rewarding success, although it is nonsense to suggest that scolding is never necessary. From the earliest age, puppies learn to understand the word, or the action implying, "No". Their mother teaches them some discipline from a very early age, and their new mother – you – needs to carry that on.

Take the common game of chewing your shoelaces. A tap on the nose while saying "No" firmly, soon teaches a puppy that there are some things in life to avoid, and that "No" means just what it says.

Similarly, most puppies start the dominance game very early in life. Nipping whomever they see as being one down from them on the totem pole quickly develops into a bite to establish their rank. Immediate remedial action – another firm "No" – will save a great deal of trauma later.

In all training there is no substitute for persistence and patience.

HOUSE TRAINING
This is the number one priority. Many puppies will not have had any house training before they arrive at their new home. They will have lived in their kennel or box with their litter mates, but even there the sleeping area is usually taboo for toileting once the puppies are old enough to move

✦ RIGHT
By eight weeks puppies should be confident and have started their house training and lead training.

around. This can be used during the course of house training.

There are two methods of teaching a puppy to use an appropriate site for its toilet, and they can be used simultaneously.

The first method involves eternal vigilance. Puppies squat to urinate and use a slightly more humped squat to defecate. As soon as the puppy postures to do either you must scoop him up and put him on the designated spot. If you miss the signs, do not scold the puppy. He doesn't yet know what he's supposed to do; he hasn't done anything wrong.

The second method is to use newspaper to cover the entire floor area on which the puppy runs. He will learn that newspaper is a suitable medium for his natural functions, and a gradual reduction in the size of the available newspaper will result in the puppy using a smaller and smaller area of floor. The theory is that you can then move the paper outside, and the puppy will continue to use it, until he learns that only outside the house is

◆ LEFT
It is important to learn the signs and to encourage the puppy by putting him outside as soon as he wakes up, and after every meal.

appropriate. Both methods work, one will suit one puppy better than another. A combination of the two by using the paper at night and extreme vigilance during the day, will usually produce the best results. Not uncommonly, older puppies may

◆ LEFT
If you are using the newspaper system for house training, it may be necessary initially to cover the entire floor.

"unlearn" about toilet training. Some trigger will cause them to break their newly formed habit. Again, please don't punish them.

This is where a dog's instinct can be useful. A healthy dog will not soil its own bed. It can be extremely helpful, for all sorts of reasons, to teach a dog to use a cage as a bed, and this is one of them. If you make it comfortable, the dog will very quickly learn to regard it as his own place to retreat to when the world gets too complicated. If the puppy does "unlearn" his house training, let him sleep in the cage, and put him out into the garden in the required place immediately after you open the cage door.

The cage mustn't be a prison for the puppy, rather a refuge, but it is useful for him to learn that sometimes the door must be shut. Suitable treats, something extra tasty, will usually persuade him to accept it.

EARLY LEAD TRAINING

1 Soft collars are more easily tolerated than new stiff leather ones.

2 Once the dog is at the stage of having a lead attached, a treat will encourage him to associate the lead with pleasure.

COMING WHEN CALLED

Your puppy will normally have an instinct to come to you from the word go. Encourage this with treats. Call the puppy by his name and, when he responds, give him a treat. It takes a very short time indeed for the puppy to associate his name with a doggy treat. But if the puppy doesn't come immediately, do not get cross and scold him. It takes an even shorter time for the puppy to learn when to run away.

GETTING USED TO A LEAD

This really must be regarded as fun by the puppy.

Step one is to put a collar on. This will feel very strange, and his immediate reaction will be to try to scratch it off. But delicious treats will distract him and overcome the itchiness of the collar.

Step two, but not until the collar is tolerated happily, is to attach a light lead. Don't hold the lead at this stage – let the puppy become accustomed to it by dragging it around. Finally, hold the lead, and gradually wind it in loosely, calling the puppy for still more treats.

3 Bribery, yet again, will take the dog's mind off the new restraint.

TRAVEL SICKNESS

Overcoming travel sickness is, or should be, a matter of early learning.

Some puppies are never travel sick, but unlike some children, those that are can nearly always be taught to overcome the problem. You must act immediately when the problem arises, otherwise the puppy starts to associate cars with vomiting, and will salivate as a premonitory symptom as soon as you put him into the car. If travel sickness is allowed to persist, the puppy will learn to hate and fear car travel.

Simply taking the puppy on plenty of short journeys may be sufficient. If the puppy learns that he can go for a ride without being sick, especially if there is a walk or a game at the end of it, he may overcome his early nervous reaction.

If the short journey cure doesn't work, there is no substitute for travel sickness pills and a much longer trip. Bear in mind that travel sickness pills take some time to be absorbed and to work. They need to be given about an

hour before the journey. To a considerable extent, the longer the journey, the more effective the treatment. Bear in mind also that most travel sickness treatments induce sleepiness, so giving the pills before going off for the family holidays can be doubly useful.

Most dogs will learn to overcome their travel sickness after a few training trips, but the longer the problem is allowed to persist before attempting a cure, the slower will be the response.

PUPPY BEHAVIOUR

Dogs are pack animals, which explains many behavioural characteristics. When you are having problems think "pack leader" and act accordingly.

One of the pack-behaviour features that all dogs bring to their relationships with human beings is hierarchy and, consequently, dominance. Puppies spend a great deal of their time trying instinctively to establish where their position is in the hierarchy, and they can only do this by attempting to establish their own dominance.

Some breeds are more dominant than others. The terriers, for instance, tend to be so; generally the gundogs do not try so hard. Being in the dominant role is not necessarily comfortable for a dog, particularly when the signals from their human companions are mixed and confusing. Most dogs settle happily in the submissive role once they are clearly placed there and learn that they do not have to attempt to keep everyone under control.

The dog's place must be established as soon as he arrives in his permanent home. He must learn that all the humans in his home are above him in the pecking order. This is not a matter of punishment for the dog. There are simple keys to make it plain.

FEEDING

The leader eats first. It is often convenient to feed the dog before you eat, but if the dog observes this, you are sending one of those confusing signals. If the family and the dog are going to eat at more or less the same time and in the same place, let the puppy wait. Puppy-feeding times are best arranged well away from your own meal times, which will avoid sending this signal. From the start, it is useful to make the

Early grooming is simply a progression from handling the dog.

puppy come to you for his food and wait until you are ready, perhaps by teaching him to sit before you put the bowl down.

GROOMING

Touching and handling are potent signals to a dog. Daily grooming under proper control will indicate who is in charge. Some puppies will resent the handling involved – dominance again – they may react as though they are being hurt. Ignore it and insist. All puppies are capable of learning very quickly whether you really mean it.

NIPPING AND BITING

Most puppies will "mouth" things, including your fingers, when they are very young. This will progress to a nip. Mouthing is normal behaviour in the young as they learn with their mouth and nose. Nipping is the first step in learning dominance. It is not amusing; stop it immediately, by a sharp reaction – the "No" it has already learned – and a tap if necessary. Remember your pack leader role!

Introduce the brush as soon as the puppy has become used to sitting quietly on the table.

GAMES AND FIGHTING

All puppies like to play games; they are part of the puppy's education, and in the light of that you should think carefully about them.

Avoid contest games with your puppy. Tug-of-war is fun, but can easily develop into a contest of dominance, with the puppy either winning the tug, or growling or snarling while hanging on. If you must play tug-of-war keep it on the very lowest key and stop immediately if the puppy starts to become too excited. Simply to stop and go away after retrieving the tug is probably as good a lesson as any.

Running after a suitably large ball (not a stick, please, or a ball small enough for the puppy to choke on) can be fun for the dog. But teach your puppy to bring the toy back to you by not running after the dog to get the ball. Show indifference if the puppy runs away with the ball, and reward him with praise and pats if he brings it back to you. You have started obedience training – congratulations!

EARLY FEEDING

1 Show the puppy his food as a preliminary to persuading him to sit.

2 The puppy has sat down, so bring him his food bowl.

3 Make the puppy wait a moment or two before allowing him to put his head into the bowl.

4 Finally the puppy gets the reward.

BASIC OBEDIENCE TRAINING

The world is a crowded place. Every dog must be able to fit into the social system around it without causing problems. Dogs may have all sorts of functions and duties, but the first, and often the only, basic necessity is that they are sufficiently trained and biddable not to cause problems for their owners. To achieve this the dog must learn basic obedience to his owner's commands.

This does not mean that the dog should be beaten into submission by a dominant owner. Apart from the cruelty of such a regime, it doesn't achieve its objective: the dog will be cowed rather than obedient, he will run away rather than respond to his owner's commands.

Basic training and obedience should be a happy experience for dog and owner. Dogs are happy to work for rewards, from a titbit to a pat on the head in praise, but they must know what you are seeking from them. Rule one is **do not confuse your dog.**

Dogs react to the immediate, not to something that happened ten minutes ago. Several other things will have happened since. Let's take as an example recalling a dog that is running free. You call him. He doesn't come back. You get cross and call him again in an angry voice, and he still doesn't come back. So you chase after him, catch him and give him a slap, or even a beating with his lead.

What does the dog learn from this? If I hear my owner calling me, I run away because if he catches me he will beat me. If I see him with the lead, I also run away because if he has the lead in his hand he uses it to beat me.

The dog shows impeccable logic in his reactions, rather than the reasoning

WALKING TO HEEL

1 Standing by his owner with a loose lead, the puppy is smelling the chance of a reward.

2 Still with a loose lead, the puppy's interest is held by the owner.

3 Moving out, the puppy stays close to his owner still with hopes of a treat.

4 Finally, the puppy has learnt that the treats will come later if he keeps by his owner's side.

that you might wish him to use. Rule two is **think like a dog**, not like a sophisticated human being.

WALKING TO HEEL

In the early learning section we explained how to accustom your young puppy to a collar and lead.

The next stage, the first in obedience, is to teach your puppy to walk on the lead without pulling. From the sight of the average dog on its lead, this is a lesson that is commonly never learned.

First steps are best taught in your own back garden or somewhere equally quiet. The puppy is already aware that a lead is attached to his collar but not that this is intended to restrain him. Pick up the lead and walk the puppy round the garden, telling him to "heel". As soon as the puppy starts to pull, simply stop and encourage him to come to you – bribes work. Do not have a tugging battle. Start moving around again, with the promise of more bribes, donkey-and-carrot style. The puppy will soon overcome his fear of the restraint. Remember, you are thinking like a dog. Trading a little restriction on freedom of movement for a choc drop (dog treat) is fair exchange.

These first steps need to be repeated for as long as it takes, but in sessions of only a few minutes. You will get bored but the puppy will not think "training session", it will think "choc-drop time".

Professional trainers often declare that bribes like treats are not to be encouraged, because they teach the dog to expect a treat whenever it does the right thing. This is true, but remember that dogs of different breeds vary in the ease with which

♦ A B O V E
The flexi lead is a useful training aid. All leads must be strong enough to restrain the dog in an emergency.

they can be trained. A Border Collie may be so anxious to please that a pat on the head is sufficient reward for any obedience success. But a terrier is a very different matter. Pats are all very well, but they don't taste as good as choc drops.

Once the puppy has overcome his fear of the restraint of the lead, some discipline does have to be introduced. Every puppy will decide that being on a lead should be challenged, and he will try an experimental pull to see what happens. This seems to be where everything goes wrong. The owner merely pulls against the dog's pull, and the dog quickly learns that the normal thing is to lean into the lead and pull the owner around behind him. This is the stage that a high proportion of dogs on leads reach.

Do not allow the pull to become established. Call the dog back to you immediately and stop walking. Praise him, yes even bribe him, when he comes back. Start again and keep the puppy on a very short lead so that he is not moving out ahead of you. Remember also that the top dog walks ahead. Who is top dog in your family?

There is something to be said for remedial training immediately if loose lead walking seems to elude you and your dog. The simplest device is the "Coke can". This is exactly what it sounds like – an empty soft drink can that has been filled with small pebbles to make a rattle. If the dog persists in pulling ahead, throw the pebble can just ahead of the dog. The surprise will often help to break the habit. Repeat as often as necessary to convince the dog that if he pulls on the lead a startling noise will occur, which has nothing to do with the ineffectual human hanging on to the lead.

A little more expensive, but a useful investment, is to buy an extending flexi lead. These are nylon leads that extend to a considerable length, unwinding from a spring-loaded handle. Many owners use them to give their dog plenty of room to roam around them on a walk, without losing control of the dog.

The lead can also be used to cure a pulling dog. Allow the dog to run out on the lead – do not pull against it – and when the dog feels that he is running free, put the brake on the

SIT

lead. It pulls the dog up suddenly. Use of the flexi lead with a normal buckled collar avoids the risk of injuring the dog. The sudden stopping action teaches the dog that his lead is there as a restraint rather than to pull against. The lesson is usually learned very quickly if accompanied by a suitable command that the dog will associate with the sudden stop to its run. Clever owners learn to use the clicking noise that the lock makes as the signal to their dog to stop in his tracks.

The choke chain has not been mentioned as a training aid for teaching walking to heel, mainly because it doesn't work until it is used so fiercely that there is danger of injury to the dog.

The choke chain and the slip lead are sometimes confused. They are two different things. The slip lead, which is usually a leather or nylon lead with a ring in one end threaded to form a noose, is a useful piece of equipment if there is a risk of the dog slipping its collar and lead. It is easily loosened, and does not have the harsh restraining action of the choke chain.

Once your dog walks to heel on a loose lead, and responds to your command to heel with reasonable alacrity, you are on your way to having an obedient dog.

SIT AND DOWN

Teaching the puppy to sit on command, and to "down", are the next practical steps for the dog owner.

As a matter of observation, if you restrain a dog in the standing position on a lead that is sufficiently short to prevent him from jumping to reach an offering, and move the offering from in front of the dog to just behind his head, the dog will sit and tip his head

1 Teaching a dog to sit starts with him standing, under control.

2 The dog has been encouraged to sit by light pressure on his haunches.

3 At a more advanced stage, hand signals may be used to instruct the dog to sit or go down.

back to try to reach the offering. Give him the sweet, and you have taught him to sit! Repeat the exercise, telling him to sit as you do so, and keep doing it until the dog has learned that "sit" means "sit for a sweet".

The "down" is an extension of the same exercise. Once your dog has learned the sit, and while keeping him under the same restraint, offer the sweet on the floor between his front paws; push the dog down at the same time telling him to "down".

All other obedience training is based on exactly these same principles, with patience and praise as the twin essentials for a happy partnership.

OBEDIENCE CLASSES

Elementary obedience lessons do not need skilled assistance, but even these can contain pitfalls for the new owner. There is an obedience class in practically every town, and it is well worthwhile for anyone with a new puppy to enquire about them. Most local obedience classes are run by experienced dog people who are only too happy to pass on their knowledge to newcomers. These obedience groups all have classes for beginners, dogs and owners, and certainly do not expect you to turn into an enthusiast for competitive dog obedience competitions. A well-trained house pet is the objective. If you get the bug and decide to join in the more advanced work, you will have started on a demanding but fascinating hobby.

An offshoot of the conventional obedience class is the ring-training class. This has much the same basis, but is intended specifically to produce well-trained show dogs. The emphasis

DOWN

1 Teaching the dog to lie follows the sit. As before, the dog is encouraged to lie down by the reward of a treat.

2 Once the dog has lowered his head, his front legs may be moved gently forward into the down position.

3 The dog is gently restrained in the down position and once again encouraged to remain there by bribery.

is on good behaviour on the lead in the presence of other dogs and a crowd of people, training the dog to allow strangers to examine it, and, one particular quirk, to stand while on the lead rather than to sit, which is the practice in obedience classes.

AGILITY AND FLYBALL COMPETITIONS

Two sports that have achieved great popularity in the United Kingdom derive directly from advanced obedience training: agility and flyball.

The **agility** competitors run an obstacle course that includes a seesaw, a tunnel, jumps, a stay on a table and weaving in-and-out obstacles. The dogs are timed, with points deducted for failure to negotiate each obstacle correctly. The requirements are strict; if the dog jumps off the seesaw before he reaches the bottom, for instance, he will lose points.

Flyball appeals to owners who want some excitement with their dogs, and if the noise coming from the flyball competition ring at Crufts dog show is anything to go by, they certainly get it. The flyball course is a short straight strip at the end of which is a box with a trap and foot lever. On a signal, the dog is released by his owner, races to the box and leaps on the foot lever, which causes a ball to fly into the air. The dog leaps to catch the ball and rushes back to his owner to give it to him or her. All is timed to the second. Flyball competitions are usually run as a relay, with four teams of six or so dogs each.

Both these activities engender great enthusiasm among their supporters and demand great dedication from the trainers and competitors.

◆ BELOW
Working dogs are trained using very similar principles.

FIELD TRIALS AND GUNDOG (SPORTING) WORKING TESTS

Field trials and gundog trials have received the status of competitions in their own right, and championships are awarded in both.

The essential difference between the two is that field trials are conducted as similarly as possible to an ordinary day's shooting of live game birds, whereas gundog trials assess the working ability of gundogs without game being shot.

Both types of trial vary in their content, depending on the breed of dog undergoing the trial. Retrievers are expected to pick up and retrieve game or the dummy; spaniels, whose job on the shooting field is to find and flush out game, are expected to quarter the ground and mark the same. Pointing is considered difficult to assess, and trials for that purpose alone are rarely held. The Springer Spaniel, which is considered the general workhorse of the shooting field, performs "hunt, point and retrieve" tests.

WORKING DOGS

From the earliest days, humans have considered their dogs to be not just companions but working allies. The dog probably came into the camps of early humans for scraps of food, the comfort of association and warmth. But it soon became apparent to the dog's host that here was a guard, warning against strangers, and on occasion, actually attacking intruders with whom it was unfamiliar.

Dogs have worked ever since. Their trainability has led to them being used over the centuries in roles varying from the simple barking burglar alarm – a role that is today recognized by some insurance companies – to out-and-out attack dogs, epitomized by the mastiff breeds, which functioned as war dogs in the Middle Ages.

Roles have been refined over the centuries, and the most important function of the majority of dogs nowadays is that of household

The Springer Spaniel, a versatile gundog, has lately come into its own as a working dog in another field, that of "sniffer". The Customs department and many police forces maintain teams of sniffer dogs to ferret out drugs being smuggled into the country, and to perform various other tasks where a keen ability to scent a suspicious substance is required. Several breeds are used, but the Springer is unsurpassed for this work.

companion, a role that is not to be underestimated.

Modern guard dogs are expected to be highly trained and totally responsive to their handler's control. The police, the prison service and the armed forces all maintain teams of dogs whose function is to guard and, if necessary, to corner an intruder or attack and bring down an assailant. It is rare for such a dog to go out of control.

There is a regular demand for young dogs to train with the services. They are looking for dogs that are bold and, in civilian owners' hands, often difficult to train. The majority of these dogs are German Shepherds, dogs that are a delight in the right hands but that may be dangerous without proper control.

Two of the oldest roles for working dogs are as livestock guards and herders, a distinction that is often misunderstood.

The Collies and various British sheepdogs have historically had a herding role. Their function is to keep the sheep flock under control at the behest of the shepherd. They circle, help move the sheep and bring strays back into the flock. Their response is to the shepherd, not the sheep.

This type of herding work depends on a carefully controlled "attack" by the dog, which runs in almost to nip the heels of the sheep, pushing it away in the direction that the shepherd calls for. Despite the shepherd's handling, the dogs learn more from their parents than from any other source.

Many of the European sheepdogs have a completely different function, acting as guards to the flock against predators. Some of the working dogs of these breeds may actually be reared

Manwork should only ever be undertaken under carefully controlled, professional supervision.

This police dog has been carefully trained to show aggression on demand when his handler requires it.

◆ LEFT
There are legal
restraints to keeping
guard dogs, intended
to avoid risks to law-
abiding citizens.

◆ ABOVE RIGHT
The Siberian Husky,
bred for the specific
purpose of pulling
sleds, makes a
delightful house
pet, given the right
environment.

◆ RIGHT
Police and Customs
dogs are widely used
for the detection of
illicit drugs.

with the sheep from an early age, growing up as one of the flock, but better equipped to ward off intruders.

These dogs, when moved out of their own working environment and into the human's, become guards of property. As with almost any breed, however, when given the right upbringing, they can make wonderful house pets for their owners.

For many years, perhaps centuries, dogs have been used as guides for blind people. The work is highly organized, by the National Guide Dogs for the Blind Association in the United Kingdom and Guiding Eyes in the United States. Guide dogs are Golden

or Labrador Retrievers, but less conventional breeds can also be trained. At least one standard Poodle has been trained to the necessary level and allocated to an applicant. The training is carried out at one of the organization's centres, and the individual dog tailored to the individual person, although sometimes applicants think it's the other way around after they have been on the introduction course!

The success of the scheme for guide dogs for the blind has encouraged enthusiasts to set up various other programmes for dogs to aid disabled people. Hearing Dogs for the Deaf is now well established in the United

Kingdom, with dogs that have learnt to alert their deaf companions when, for instance, the front door bell rings.

One of the most successful schemes is Pat Dogs or Pet Partners. These are companion dogs whose owners take them to hospitals and hospices to visit the patients. Many people miss their own dog, or find comfort just from having a dog to talk to and stroke while they are in hospital. The therapeutic effect on the patients is demonstrable. Any breed is suitable, though not every dog; they must be dogs that enjoy human company but don't demonstrate their enjoyment too effusively.

The Harrier, one of the oldest breeds of hunting dog, has never been included in the Kennel Club registers.

Tracking, sometimes to search for criminals but often to seek out people or objects that may be lost, is another specialist duty of the ubiquitous German Shepherd.

BEHAVIOUR PROBLEMS

Behaviour problems develop because the dog has received signals that the type of behaviour now regarded as a problem has been acceptable, up to now. This nearly always arises because we give conflicting signs to the dog.

Take sitting on the sofa. If you allow a sweet little puppy up on to your lap, how is he to know that when he gets bigger he can't do it? Until one

♦ ABOVE
Chewing of household objects may arise simply from boredom or separation anxiety.

♦ LEFT
Jumping up is probably the commonest objectionable behaviour by dogs. It is far better prevented than cured.

day you push him off, and there is a confrontation.

Curing behaviour problems is much more difficult than preventing them. Obedience training has a considerable role in overcoming potential behavioural problems, and many enthusiasts have developed their interest through the need to create a reasonably well-behaved pet.

DOMINANCE
The development of dominance is by far the most common cause of real problems. Dominant behaviour will lead to biting. Often enough, the dog will have learned that one or more of the family is in the pack leader's position, but that some, often the children, appear to be below the dog in the pecking order.

Dominance cannot always be cured, but it can usually be controlled, provided the whole family co-operates. The method is to re-establish the order of dominance in the pack.

Rule one is never to confront the dog unless you know you can win. A dominant dog becomes aggressive in order to protect his position. His bite is often worse than your bark.

Start by totally ignoring the dog, and that must include all the members of your family. Almost always the dog

reassert his own dominance – don't allow him into your bedroom, for instance. Keep him strictly off chairs and that sofa. Physical height, achieved by getting on to chairs, is a dominance signal, and sitting on a chair may be sufficient to indicate to your dog that he has made himself tops.

You don't need to be in any hurry to take the trailing lead away. This gives you a lot of control without risk to yourself. Games must be entirely in your control. You start them and you stop them, and above all avoid confrontational games that the dog can feel he has won. At the same time

will very soon approach you for attention. Make sure he doesn't get it. Put a long lead on as soon as you can do so safely, and leave it to trail. Use the lead to make the dog do what you want him to.

If the problem has been that he won't get off the sofa without growling at you, pull him off from a distance. You are beginning to re-assert your authority.

Re-establish the feeding regime – make the dog wait, and then make him

approach you for his food rather than taking the food to him. Then ignore him again.

Stop greeting the dog. If he wants attention, he must come to you, and then be rebuffed until you have decided that he has behaved well enough to relax your attitude a little. He must be given no opportunity to

Aggression needs professional attention. It may have several causes.

◆ LEFT
All dogs enjoy foraging in dustbins. If you don't want the dog to get at the dustbin, put it out of reach.

AGGRESSION TOWARDS GUESTS

1 Aggression towards guests is often a defensive or fear reaction.

2 Letting the dog realize that guests are not intruders may often be accomplished with a suitable treat.

as you are asserting the new regime, it is essential that the rest of the family behave in exactly the same way.

Most dogs never exhibit dominance problems; if they did they wouldn't be such popular companions for humans, but when a dog does start to show signs of dominant behaviour he must be controlled totally, or it will lead to trouble, and trouble means biting, humans or other dogs.

If you do not seem to be able to control incipient dominance, or aggression, quickly by these simple rules, take professional advice before the problem becomes serious.

FEAR BITING

A high proportion of unacceptable behaviour involves the dog biting someone. Aggression that arises from dominance accounts for much of this, but fear biting occurs regularly in less dominant dogs. The only way a dog has of protecting himself is to bite his perceived attacker or to run away. Fear biting will occur if the dog cannot run away.

Fear of the unknown is usually the problem. If a dog does not meet many

3 Overcoming this type of aggression is easier with a well-trained dog that can be kept under restraint.

people as a puppy, he may, depending on his natural disposition, regard people as a whole as the unknown and react accordingly. Early training will nearly always prevent this reaction. If early contacts are insufficient and the

dog is nervous of people he does not know, there is no substitute for slow and careful broadening of the dog's circle of acquaintances, until he has met so many people that nobody seems to be a stranger. The same approach must

◆ BELOW
A dog which doesn't come when called means back to square one.

be taken if a puppy takes fright at cars, for instance. Non-confrontational acquaintance with his particular fear object will cure the problem.

BARKING FOR ATTENTION
It is not unknown for a dog to use a fear reaction as an attention-getter. If a

puppy learns that barking at an object, any object, will result in his owner giving him all sorts of comforting attention, he will very quickly realize that if he wants attention, he should bark, and preferably in an alarmed fashion for an instant response.

ODD PROBLEMS
You may think you cannot win, but we all tolerate a certain amount of

contrariness in our dogs. Nobody's perfect, and it's part of their charm.

There are other, more bizarre, behavioural problems that usually do not involve actual risk to the owner. One of the commoner of these problems is the dog that tears the house to pieces when the owner goes

◆ LEFT
It is natural for dogs to howl like their cousin the wolf. In domestic circumstances howling is usually a sign of distress.

◆ BELOW
Decide early what is tolerable in the way of begging for titbits, and stick to it.

out. It doesn't help just to say that this is another anxiety manifestation. Sometimes the reasons are complex, and the cure always demands considerable commitment on the part of the owner. It should always be undertaken with the supervision of an expert animal behaviourist.

Health Care and First Aid

In order to recognize when a dog is ill, you must know
the signs of good health. A healthy dog is alert and lively, and takes a great
interest in its environment, although young puppies will be, quite normally,
rushing about one minute and sound asleep the next. There should be no
discharges from the eyes or nose. The nose is usually moist and shiny, but this
will depend on what the dog has been doing – people are often concerned that
their dog's nose is dry, when all that has happened is that he has been digging
for his favourite bone! The ears should be clean and free of visible wax.
The coat should be free of dandruff and, depending on the coat type, more
or less shiny. The skin should be free from sores or spots.The dog should
move soundly, that is to say without favouring one leg over another, and
he should move freely. A healthy dog should have a healthy appetite.
He should be ready for his food, and eat it with relish.

♦ FACING PAGE
Vets' surgeries are
usually relaxed places
and visiting one
should not cause
your dog any stress.

INTRODUCING YOUR DOG TO THE VETERINARY SURGEON

Ideally, if you have not previously owned an animal, you should make the acquaintance of your local veterinary surgeon before you acquire the dog. How you choose a vet is a matter of personal preference. You may be guided by friends, or the convenience of the surgery, but there is no substitute for a personal interview to get an idea of how the practice runs, its surgery times and facilities, all of which the veterinary surgeon will be pleased to discuss with you.

Within twenty-four hours you and your family are going to have grown very attached to your puppy. That is just the way it happens. It is important

that, if the veterinary examination discovers anything that indicates the puppy should be returned to the seller, you should know immediately before this bonding has taken place. So you must arrange for the puppy's examination to take place on the day you collect him.

The veterinary surgeon will repeat the superficial health checks that you will already have carried out before buying the dog, but will go into greater detail, with a check on the puppy's heart and lungs, his ears and skin, his legs and feet and his genito-urinary system as far as possible.

This examination should not alarm the puppy. The veterinary surgeon will spend time getting to know your new dog with a little friendly fussing to give him confidence, before making the more detailed examination.

Almost certainly, unless he has already received his first inoculation, he will be given it now. Again, this should not alarm the puppy, and many don't even notice the injection. At worst there may be a squeak, followed by some more comforting. The whole event should be very low key.

The veterinary surgeon will also probably advise on worming and anti-flea regimes, and tell you how long it must be before the puppy meets other dogs in order to give the vaccine a chance to develop the dog's immunity to infections.

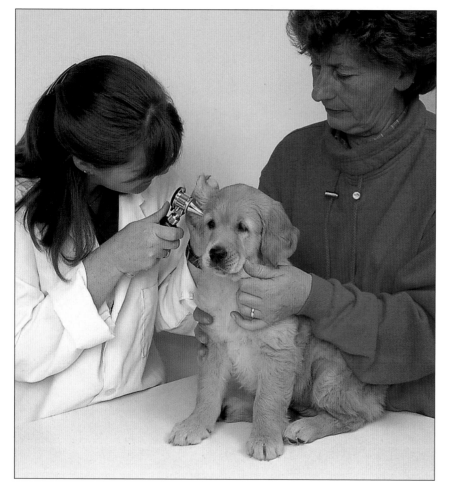

◆ ABOVE
Minimum restraint is important in encouraging your dog to relax at the surgery.

◆ LEFT
Most dogs, if handled with confidence, will not require heavy restraint during veterinary procedures.

THE INOCULATION REGIME

The dog's inoculations cover a core of four major diseases: distemper, which includes hardpad; leptospirosis, a liver and kidney infection; hepatitis, caused by a liver virus; and parvovirus. Kennel cough vaccine may also be included at a puppy's primary vaccination stage.

The first component of the vaccination course is usually given at seven to eight weeks old, although in circumstances where there has been a perceived risk in the breeder's kennels, much earlier protection may be given against certain diseases. Such very early vaccinations are usually disregarded for the purposes of routine protection.

The second injection is given at around twelve weeks of age. The interval between vaccinations is necessary to allow the puppy's immune system to react properly to the first dose of vaccine; the second dose then boosts the level of immunity to such an extent that the dog is protected for a prolonged period.

The vaccines are repeated annually, a process known as "boosters". Owners are inclined to be lax in their response to booster reminders as the dog gets older. Don't! Although some elements of the dog vaccination programme may confer a solid immunity for life, this cannot be relied upon, and other elements definitely need boosting annually.

LIFELONG IMMUNIZATION

Some infections in dogs are unlikely to strike the dog more than once in its lifetime. Vaccination against these diseases may confer a lifelong immunity. The virus hepatitis of the dog is one of these diseases.

BOOSTER INOCULATIONS

Unfortunately other infections, although again unlikely to affect the dog more than once, do not confer such a solid immunity for life, although the immunity that they do confer is excellent for as long as it lasts. Typical of this group is distemper and hardpad (which is caused by the same virus). Distemper vaccinations must be boosted about every second year to maintain a high level of immunity.

There is a third group of infections that may recur and to which the immunity offered by vaccination is relatively short-lived. It is still worthwhile to use the vaccine because of the dangerous nature of the illness. Such a disease is leptospirosis, transmitted usually by foxes or other dogs, but occasionally, in the case of one type of the disease, by rats.

Not all diseases to which dogs are susceptible can be avoided by vaccination, but the commonest killers certainly can.

KENNEL COUGH

A particular problem for which there is no total preventive control is kennel cough, an infectious inflammation of the larynx and trachea. Kennel cough may be an unfair description. The disease is transmitted by droplets coughed into the air by dogs actively suffering from the illness. Fairly close contact between dogs is necessary for its transmission, such as a nose-to-nose greeting through the wire by dogs in kennels. At least as common a cause is dogs meeting at shows, competitions or training classes.

Kennel cough is caused by a mixture of infectious agents. The most effective vaccine, although it still does not include every possible component of the infection, is given as a nasal spray. Most kennels advise owners to make sure their dogs have had a kennel cough vaccination shortly before going into kennels. Some insist before accepting the dog. The advice is sensible.

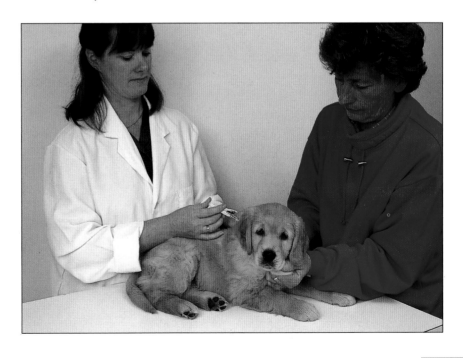

WORM CONTROL

Dogs are prone to both internal and external parasitic infestations. There are two common worms in dogs: the tapeworm and the roundworm.

TAPEWORMS

Tapeworms may affect dogs at any age, although they are less common in young puppies than in older dogs. The tapeworm has a life cycle that depends on two different host species, in the case of the most frequently seen worm, the dog and the dog's fleas, although in another species they are transmitted through sheep.

Tapeworms may be recognizable as "rice grains" in the faeces, but the dog may give you an indication by undue attention to its anal region.

Control of the tapeworm in the dog is simple; modern treatments are straightforward, requiring no fasting before dosing, and highly effective, with very little in the way of side-effects (occasional vomiting).

It is a good idea to treat your dog routinely against tapeworms every six months. However, prevention of re-infection depends on control of the flea population in your house.

ROUNDWORMS

Roundworms are practically universal in puppies. They may be transmitted directly from dog to dog by faecal contamination, which is almost impossible to avoid. A high proportion of puppies are actually born infected with roundworms, transmitted via the uterus of the mother. Worms that had lain dormant in the tissues of the dam are activated by the hormones produced during pregnancy, circulate in the mother's bloodstream and pass into the unborn

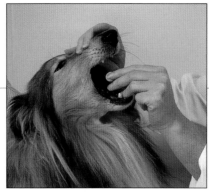

Any tablet needs to be given right to the back of the dog's mouth. Wrap it in something pleasant to distract him from spitting it out.

pups. There are control regimes that depend on using a safe anthelmintic early in pregnancy to destroy the maternal worm load, but this treatment is by no means universal.

A proper rearing regime will include dosing the litter when it is three or four weeks old, and perhaps again before leaving the kennels. Once in your home the puppy should be treated regularly, according to your veterinary surgeon's advice, every three to four weeks until it is six months old.

Adult dogs build up a level of immunity to the effects of roundworm infestations, and after six months do not need such regular treatment. Keep a constant look-out, although roundworms are not always easy to detect in a dog's faeces.

A dog will eat grass when his stomach is upset, but many dogs simply enjoy a little grazing.

WORM TREATMENTS

There are drug treatments that are effective against tapeworms and roundworms in one dose. One possibility is to give older dogs this type of treatment once every six months. The ascarid roundworm may be the cause of a very rare eye condition in children. If the dog is regularly wormed, the risk, already remote, is eliminated. With this exception, the worms of dogs and of humans are not transmissible.

Other species of worms, including the hookworm, may occur in dogs. Treatment is not difficult, but diagnosis may not be straightforward. Consult your veterinary surgeon. In the United States, heartworm is a common problem. A preventive medicine is given orally; treatment can be costly, and dangerous for the dog.

◆ RIGHT
All dogs will lick and clean their anal region, but frequent licking is a sign that veterinary attention is needed.

EXTERNAL PARASITES

FLEAS

Start by assuming that your dog has fleas! They are by far the commonest external parasite of the dog. A high proportion of skin problems may be caused, directly or indirectly, by their presence.

Fleas thrive in the warm and cosy environment of a centrally heated house, and there is no longer a flea season in summer followed by a flea-free winter. Treatment should be continued all through the year.

Fleas are often difficult to diagnose. They are small, move rapidly and are able to hop considerable distances. They are not very easy to see on the dog, but they never live alone. If you see one flea it is safe to assume that there are plenty more. If you see none at all, they are probably still somewhere around.

A useful home test is to scrape hair detritus on to newspaper, and then to dampen the paper. If red smears appear it is a certain indication that the dog does have fleas. The detritus may look like coal dust, but it is flea excreta.

Once you have convinced yourself that even your dog may have fleas, treatment is straightforward, although control is anything but. There are several effective sprays and washes available that will kill fleas safely (but some for which care is necessary), and most have some residual effect. But re-infestation is very difficult to prevent. If protection is, say, for three months, in practice the effectiveness is likely to decline well within that time. So some fleas come back.

Recent advances have been made with non-toxic preparations to be given to the dog monthly in tablet form. These do not kill adult fleas but

act by breaking the flea's breeding cycle. All flea treatments are demanding in that they must be given regularly if they are to work.

The important thing to remember is that fleas leave the host to

◆ RIGHT
Scratching is normal, but persistent scratching demands attention. In nine out of ten cases it will be something as simple as fleas.

reproduce, and that for every flea you find on the dog, there are literally thousands in your dog's bed, in the nooks and crannies in the floor, in the carpets, between the cushions on the sofa, all breeding away like mad.

✦ BELOW
The Elizabethan collar is extremely useful to prevent self-mutilation around the head. The cause of the inflammation must be determined.

There are a number of preparations on the market that provide effective protection around the house. Thorough vacuuming of the carpets helps but will not overcome the problem. Flea eggs, laid in their thousands, are able to survive for long periods in a warm environment. Disturbance causes the eggs to hatch, in itself a reason for regular vacuum cleaning, as the eggs in their shells are resistant to insecticides.

TICKS

Ticks tend to be a country dog problem. Their usual host is the sheep. In the United States, Australia, South Africa and the tropics, ticks transmit certain rapidly fatal diseases to dogs, and the dogs are routinely dipped or sprayed against infestation, often on a weekly basis. This is not necessary in Europe, where tick-borne disease is uncommon in the dog.

Ticks engorge on the blood of their host; the engorged tick is sometimes mistaken for a wart on the dog's skin.

Dogs will occasionally pick up a solitary tick, but may sometimes be seen to have several. Adult female ticks lay groups of eggs, which hatch at more or less the same time to form a colony of young ticks attached to grass stems waiting to find a host. If a dog comes by, several of the "seed ticks" may attach themselves to him.

The ticks are usually removed individually. Do not try to pick them off. That's rarely successful, and there are various substances that will kill them. Ear drops that are intended to destroy parasites are useful as is methylated spirit, or even gin! The tick will not fall off immediately but it should have disappeared twelve hours

after application. Most anti-flea preparations will also kill them.

In the United States, Lyme disease is transmitted by ticks that live on deer and mice, and is a serious threat to dogs. Fortunately, a vaccine is available.

LICE

Fortunately lice are now uncommon parasites of the dog. Lice are detectable by the presence of just

visible groups of eggs attached to the hair, often of the ears or head of the dog. Lice are small and are not mobile. They tend to occur in large numbers, but do not seem to be as itchy to the dog as fleas.

Lice are transmitted directly from dog to dog by contact. They are not transmitted to humans or to other animals. They may be controlled by the use of insecticidal shampoos.

SIGNS OF ILLNESS

One of the first signs that a dog is ill is if he refuses his food. Most fussy dogs will at least smell the food on offer, but a sick dog may have no appetite and simply not approach his food.

The dog will tend to become duller than usual, although many sick dogs will still respond to their owner's enthusiasm for a game or a walk.

ACUTE ILLNESS
The term "acute" does not necessarily mean a serious illness. When your

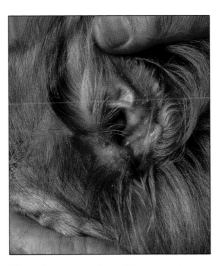

The ear is an extremely sensitive organ. Any inflammation demands immediate attention from the veterinary surgeon.

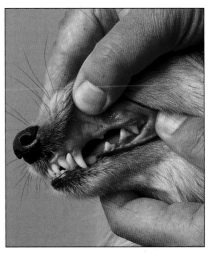

Dogs on modern diets are inclined to acquire tartar on their teeth, which needs attention if it is not to lead on to more serious problems.

SIGNS OF ACUTE ILLNESS

Tense, swollen stomach. A drum-like swelling of the abdomen an hour or two after feeding, accompanied by obvious distress with panting and salivation, may indicate that the dog has bloat. This is an emergency.

Vomiting several times, particularly if it persists for more than twelve hours. Vomiting once or twice is common, and a normal reaction to eating something unsuitable. Some dogs eat grass, appearing to do it to make themselves sick. If this happens occasionally, there is probably nothing to worry about. Persistent vomiting after eating grass may suggest an acute problem.

Diarrhoea persisting for twenty-four hours or longer. Diarrhoea will often accompany vomiting. If the faeces are bloodstained, treatment may be needed urgently.

Difficulty breathing, gasping, choking.

Collapse, loss of consciousness, fits.

Each of these conditions needs immediate attention from your veterinary surgeon.

---

veterinary surgeon refers to an acute illness he simply means one that has come on rapidly, whereas a "chronic" illness is one that is long lasting and has appeared gradually.

Young puppies are occasionally subject to fits, from which they usually recover quickly. Observe the fit carefully so that you can describe it when you get to the vet's. Did the dog just collapse silently, did it squeal or howl, did it paddle its legs, did it urinate or defaecate during the fit? Once a dog has recovered from a fit it may be very difficult for the veterinary surgeon to be precise about the cause; there may be nothing for him to see.

Other signs of acute illness include serious bleeding, or bleeding from any orifice (see First Aid); obvious pain, indicated by noise (squealing, crying, yelping on movement), lameness, or tenderness to touch; straining to pass faeces, or inability to pass urine; any obvious severe injury, or swelling on the body; a closed eye, or inflammation with excessive tears; violent

scratching or rubbing, particularly around the ears or head.

CHRONIC ILLNESS
The signs of chronic illness appear gradually and are likely to be more subtle and difficult to recognize.

Loss of weight, persisting over a period of weeks, is a common indicator of chronic disease. This may be accompanied by a normal or reduced appetite.

Gradually developing swellings may indicate the growth of superficial tumours, often not cancerous but usually needing attention.

Other signs include hair loss, with or without sore skin or itching and scratching; slowly developing lameness; excessive drinking, with or without an unpleasant odour from the mouth or body. Occasional vomiting may indicate an internal problem, although many healthy dogs may also vomit. In the normal course of events, bitches may frequently regurgitate food for their puppies.

FIRST AID FOR YOUR DOG

♦ BELOW
Sores and rashes may develop beneath a long coat for some time before they become obvious.

First-aid treatments may be divided into problems that you can deal with yourself, and treatments to carry out to keep the problem to a minimum before you take the dog to the veterinary surgeon.

SORES AND RASHES

A dog may get a sore place or a rash through chewing itself. Many dogs will chew their skin raw if there is an itch. The dog may get a rash from insect bites – typically flea bites, from skin contact with irritants such as nettles, or as an allergic response to an external or internal substance. It is often difficult to tell to what extent the sore area is caused by

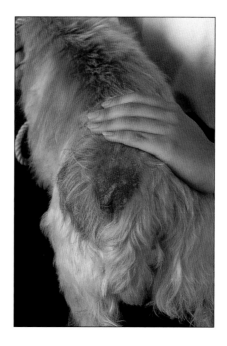

the irritant or is self-inflicted as a result of the irritation.

The object of treatment, whether your own first aid or your veterinary surgeon's, is to eliminate the cause before attempting to cure the effect.

If a dog has been scratching itself a little more than usual, the commonest cause is the presence of fleas. Fleas never come singly. If you see a flea, there will definitely be others. One or two may be sufficient to start the itch cycle off. The answer is to treat the fleas (see External Parasites), and the problem will usually disappear. If it doesn't, a soothing cream, such as rescue cream, will be sufficient.

FIRST-AID KIT

The most important item in your first-aid kit should be your veterinary surgeon's name and telephone number. Even though you may have it else-where, it doesn't harm to duplicate it.

Absorbent cotton wool

Adhesive and gauze bandages, 5cm (2in) and 10cm (4in)

Gauze swabs, sterile wraps

Cotton buds

Scissors, sharp-pointed

Thermometer

Forceps, medium-sized, blunt points

Plastic syringe, 20ml (½fl oz)

Eye drops

Cleansing ear drops

Antiseptic or antibiotic ointment

Antiseptic powder and wash

Rescue cream

Medicinal liquid paraffin

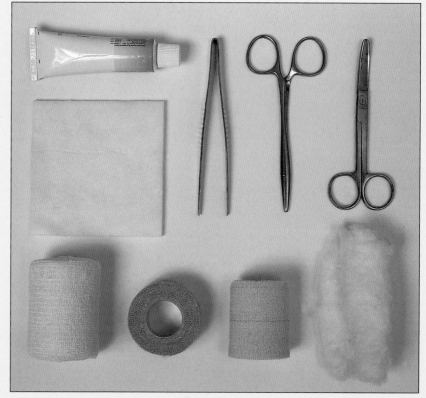

The forceps in a first-aid kit should never be used for probing around.
You must always be able to see whatever it is you are attempting to remove.

TAKING TEMPERATURE

1 First, shake the thermometer so that the level of mercury is well below the expected temperature of the dog.

2 Slide the lubricated thermometer carefully into the dog's anus and press lightly against the side of the rectum.

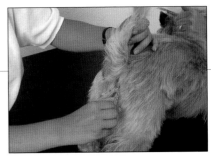

3 The thermometer should be held in place for at least sixty seconds before reading.

BANDAGING A PAW

1 First, pad the leg with cotton-wool strips between the toes.

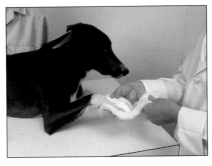

2 Place a generous amount of further padding over the end of the foot to cushion it before starting to bandage.

3 The bandage must always include the foot and be extended above the wound.

4 Bandage the leg firmly, but take care that the bandage is not so tight that circulation is restricted.

5 Tie the bandage off well above the site of the wound.

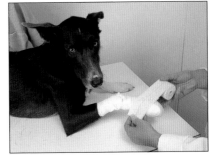

6 Cover the whole of the bandage in an adhesive dressing, firmly but not tightly, and secure it at the back of the dog's leg.

CUTS AND SCRATCHES

Treatment depends on how large and how deep the cut or scratch is. The dog's skin does not usually bleed profusely, and it is easy to miss even quite a large cut because there may be very little bleeding and the dog's fur covers the site.

If there is any sign of blood on the dog, look carefully and once you have located the cut, clip sufficient hair around it to expose the wound. If the cut looks deep, or longer than about 1cm (½in), it will need attention and, probably, a stitch or two at the veterinary surgery.

If you decide to take the dog to the vet, do nothing with the wound, unless it is bleeding profusely. The nurse is likely to take longer cleaning your dressing off the wound than the stitching itself will take.

A minor cut, or a scratch that does not penetrate the skin, will usually need very little treatment. Soothing cream will be sufficient, and even that may do more to prolong healing than to help, by bringing the attention of the dog to the wound.

Similarly, a small cut needs no particular attention once you have trimmed the hair away, other than to keep the wound clean with a mild antiseptic solution, and to keep an eye open for any swelling. Swelling may indicate that an infection has set in.

BITES

Dog bites will often become infected. This is particularly the case when the bite causes a puncture wound. Unless the wounds are multiple, or large enough obviously to require veterinary attention, there is no emergency, but the dog should be taken to the veterinary surgery within twenty-four hours to allow the vet to assess whether antibiotic injections are needed. Prior to that, the wound may be cleansed with antiseptic lotion.

BLEEDING

Treatment will depend on how heavily the wound is bleeding. Skin wounds may only need cleansing, followed by the application of a little antiseptic cream and a careful eye on the progress of the wound. It will probably stop bleeding in a short time.

Profuse bleeding is an emergency, usually indicating a wound that is sufficiently deep to need urgent veterinary attention. Steps to control the bleeding while on the way to the surgery are worthwhile, and may be life-saving. Tourniquets are no longer used, do not attempt to make one. Use a pressure bandage over the wound.

The rare need for a pressure bandage is one reason for the cotton wool and bandages in your first-aid kit. When needed, take a large wad of cotton wool, as large as is available in your kit. Place it directly over the wound, and bandage firmly. If the wound is on a limb, bandage right down to the foot and include the entire leg below the wound in your bandage. Make sure the site over the wound is firmly bandaged, and take the dog to the surgery.

HEAT STROKE

1 First signs of heat stroke are obvious distress and incessant panting.

2 The dog should be cooled immediately by sponging or hosing down with cold water. Ensure that the head is drenched.

HEAT EXHAUSTION

Some breeds of dog are more prone to heat exhaustion than others – Chow Chows and Bulldogs come to mind, but several other short-nosed breeds can also be affected.

The most common reason for heat exhaustion is human error. Dogs are too often left inside cars in summer without adequate ventilation. The owner is usually just thoughtless, or caught out by a change in the weather during a longer than expected shopping trip. The temperature inside a closed car in summer in even a temperate climate can kill a dog. Many have died in this way. The signs of heat stress are obvious distress,

BANDAGING AN EAR

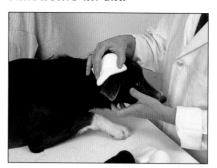

1 Ears are often damaged in dog fights and can bleed profusely. Clean the wound, then place an absorbent pad behind the dog's affected ear.

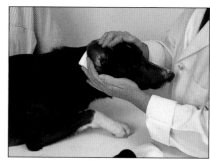

2 Carefully fold the ear back on to the pad.

BANDAGING A TAIL

1 Successful tail bandaging is fraught with difficulty. First enclose the tail lengthways in a bandage.

2 Lay strips of bandage along the length of the tail.

3 A wet towel, frequently changed, will help to cool the dog down and in a hot environment may help to prevent heat stroke.

heavy panting, and an inability to breathe deeply enough indicated by a half strangled noise coming from the dog's throat. The dog's tongue looks swollen and blue.

Treat as an immediate emergency, and do not attempt to take the dog for veterinary treatment until you have started its resuscitation. Plenty of cold water is the first-aid treatment.

Ideally, immerse the whole dog in a bath – use a cattle trough if there is one nearby. Bathe the dog all over with cold water, but especially drench its head; and keep doing it until the dog shows signs of easier breathing. Then take it to the veterinary surgeon. The vet will possibly put the dog on to an oxygen air flow, and will probably give it an injection to reduce the swelling in its throat, but unless the vet happens to be at hand, as he may be at a dog show, the life-saving treatment will have been given before the dog gets to the surgery.

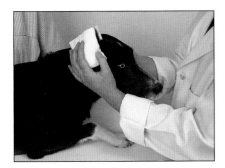

3 Place the pad over the folded back ear.

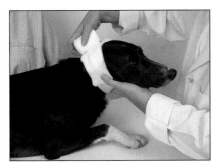

4 Start bandaging around the neck from behind the ear and work forward, enclosing the affected ear, not too tightly.

5 The unaffected ear should not be included in the bandaging.

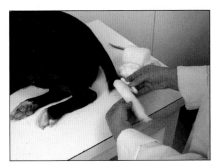

3 Bandage the tail around its length, whenever possible including some of the dog's tail hair within the turns of the bandage.

4 Cover the bandage with an adhesive dressing.

5 Take the adhesive dressing well above the end of the bandage and include strands of hair within each turn.

EXAMINING AND BRUSHING TEETH

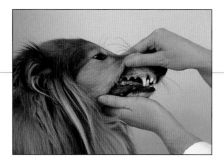

1 Regular brushing will slow up the formation of plaque and tartar.

2 Some dogs will resent the use of a brush, but toothpaste on the end of a finger can be almost as effective.

3 Specially made dog toothbrushes are often well tolerated.

EXAMINING EYES

1 Take great care when administering eye drops or ointment. It is important to hold the dog's eyelids open so that the medication actually goes into the eyes.

2 After the drops have been put in, the eyelids must be gently massaged over the surface of the eye to encourage the spread of the medication.

Sick dogs must be kept warm, dry and comfortable. They may be encouraged to eat but never force-fed. The dog should always have easy access to water.

SNAKE BITES, AND STINGS FROM OTHER VENOMOUS CREATURES

These are often difficult to recognize unless the bite is witnessed. The degree of urgency depends on the type of venomous creature, where on its body the dog was bitten, and the age of the dog. Small puppies are obviously more at risk than older, larger animals.

The only venomous British snake is the adder. The risk is greater in areas with certain types of soil – sandy downs seem to harbour more adders than most other areas. In the United States, Australia and Africa the most common snake bites in dogs are from the viperine snakes. Poisonous North American snakes include rattlesnakes and coral snakes.

Snakes are often more likely to bite when they come out to sun themselves on a warm spring day, and the dog goes to investigate. So the dog is most likely to be bitten on the face, head or neck.

If the dog's face starts to swell up while you are out on a walk, the chance of a snake bite must be considered. Unless the swelling starts to cause obvious breathing distress, treatment is urgent, but this is not a life-threatening emergency. You can afford to walk back to the car, no need to run, but make sure the dog walks quietly – exercise should be minimal. Carry a

Disturb an injured dog as little as possible, although be prepared to lift it carefully and take it to a veterinary surgeon immediately.

small dog. Take the dog straight to the surgery. Very few dogs in Britain die from the effects of adder venom, but many each year have distressing abscesses caused by a combination of the venom and infection.

Bites from non-venomous snakes should be thoroughly cleaned as the snake's teeth may be carrying bacteria, which could cause infection.

The only reason to include snake bites in the first aid section is that there is a belief that the venom of a snake should be "sucked out" of the wound. Do not attempt to do so.

Bee and wasp stings carry a similar risk of death to snake bites – generally, they are only likely to be lethal if the swelling from the bite blocks the dog's airway. The exception to this is the case of multiple stings, the shock of which can cause the death of the dog. Such events are rare.

Venomous spiders are unknown in the United Kingdom and uncommon in the United States, although they do occur there. The Australian funnel spider, however, is an extremely venomous arachnid.

A single swelling from a bee or wasp sting does not usually require veterinary treatment, but home attention with a soothing cream will speed the dog's recovery, and possibly stop the "sore scratch" cycle.

CHOKING

Some dogs are inveterate pickers up of sticks and stones, or ball chasers. All carry the risk of getting an object stuck in the mouth or throat. A half swallowed ball may be an emergency by reason of a blocked airway. First aid may be a two-handed job. You could get bitten. If the dog seems to

be choking, look in his mouth with care. A block of wood to prevent him closing his teeth over your fingers can help, with one person holding the dog's head while the other looks into his mouth. If there is a ball in the dog's throat, try to lever it out with a fine rod rather than with your hand.

A frequent occurrence is that a piece of wood becomes wedged across the teeth, or between the back teeth. Treat removal with similar caution, using some sort of lever to remove it. This type of incident not infrequently requires a trip to the vet and sedation to remove the object.

WHAT TO DO IN A ROAD ACCIDENT INVOLVING A DOG

It is virtually certain that a dog involved in a road accident will not be under control. The first step, even before looking to see what may be wrong, is to leash the dog with whatever comes to hand. But you must do it without risk to yourself.

A noose needs to be made and slipped over the dog's head without actually touching the dog. The noose

may be easily made from your own dog's lead or any other line or even a piece of string.

The next step, unless the dog is obviously unconscious, is to muzzle the dog. Any dog that has been involved in a road accident is likely to be in shock, and even the

Many road accidents and injuries to dogs may be avoided if the owner exercises the dog sensibly by restraining it with a lead.

◆ RIGHT
Large injured dogs may be carried with one arm at the front of their chest, under the neck, and the other looped through to allow the back legs to hang. A muzzle may be necessary.

Despite the first-aid warning about not moving an injured person, you are better to take the dog straightaway to the veterinary surgery than to wait while someone phones around to find a vet who can leave the surgery to attend the accident. There is no organized emergency ambulance service for animals.

Once the dog's mouth is bound and it cannot bite, it is almost always safe to carry the dog. If possible, let the affected leg hang free – you will avoid further damage, and pain.

Dogs in road accidents will often run away, despite serious injury. If you see this happen, warn the police, who will at least be able to inform anyone who enquires about their missing dog.

Sometimes the police will accept immediate responsibility for the care of dogs involved in road accidents. If they are informed of an accident and are able to attend the scene, they will usually know the local veterinary surgeons and be able to advise on the vet's phone numbers.

most friendly can bite whoever is attending it, through pain or through fear.

You are unlikely to be carrying a proper muzzle with you. Once again, a cord, or a dog lead, or a bandage can be used. Only once the dog is secure, and you are unlikely to be bitten, should you try to examine the dog.

If the dog is not conscious, do not try to resuscitate it – get it to the veterinary surgery as quickly as possible. If other people are there, ask

someone to phone ahead to the surgery to warn them that you are coming.

A coat or blankets may be used as a makeshift stretcher, but only a dog that is so badly injured that it is unaware of its surroundings is likely to tolerate being carried in this way.

If the dog is bleeding heavily, use whatever is available to make a pressure pad; bind the wound and take the dog to the surgery immediately.

If the dog is carrying a leg, or is limping, there may be a fracture.

MUZZLING AN INJURED DOG

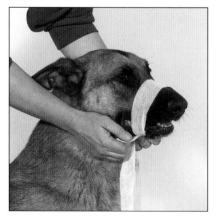

1 An improvised muzzle may be made with a bandage or almost any material. Make a loop, pass it over the dog's muzzle and under its chin.

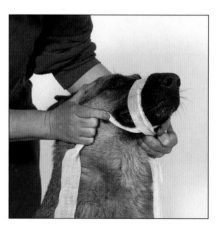

2 Take the ends of the material behind the dog's ears.

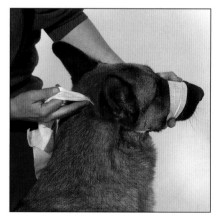

3 Tie the muzzle firmly behind the dog's head. An improvised muzzle must be tied tightly. It will not choke the dog.

POISONING AND COMMON POISONS

The poisons likely to be encountered by a dog are almost always those found around the house and garden. They include tablets and medicines intended for human consumption, or not for internal use at all, household chemicals such as bleach or detergents, and garden chemicals.

Puppies will try anything. You must keep all potentially dangerous materials out of their reach, preferably in a locked cupboard.

If an accident does occur, and you think your dog has eaten something that could be poisonous, there are two things to do.

1 Make the dog sick. If this is to be of any help, it must be done before the poisonous substance has had a chance to be absorbed from the stomach, so do it before contacting your veterinary surgeon. But if you know your vet is immediately available for advice, and you are certain what it is the dog has

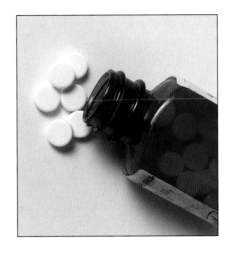

eaten, do not make the dog sick until you have spoken.

The most effective substance to use to make the dog sick is washing soda. Put two small crystals on to the back of the dog's tongue, and make him swallow them by holding his mouth shut and stroking his throat. Vomiting

will take place within minutes so be prepared with old newspapers at hand.

2 Contact your veterinary surgeon. Retain some of the poisonous substance, or at least its wrapping, to show him or her. There may be no ill effect, or immediate further treatment may be necessary.

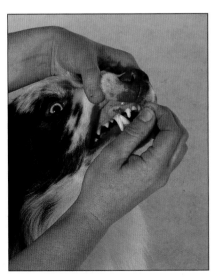

Do not make the dog vomit if the toxic substance is already being absorbed, which occurs within thirty or so minutes of ingestion.

SOME COMMON POISONS

Rat poisons – all rat poisons are coloured to indicate the active substance. They are of low toxicity to dogs when used properly, but dogs may get hold of bulk quantities.
Blue: Anticoagulants
Brown: Calciferol
Green: Alphachloralose
Pink or Grey: Gamma-HCH (Lindane)
  If rat poisoning is suspected, the package or some of the suspect material must be retained for examination by the veterinary surgeon.

Barbiturates – human sleeping pills.

Sodium Chlorate – weed killer.

Detergents – usually safe, but if concentrated may cause external lesions, or vomiting if swallowed.

Antifreeze – Ethylene glycol.

Lead – old paint chewed by dogs.

Slug bait – metaldehyde, attractive to dogs, now has anti-dog component.

Cigar and cigarette ends – nicotine.

Organochlorine, Organophosphorus compounds – flea and lice killers.

Paraquat – herbicide.

Aspirin – taken in large quantity.

Strychnine – vermin killer, dogs may get at carcasses.

Toad – from mouthing the toad. Exotic toads are more venomous.

Tranquillizers.

INHERITED DISEASES

An inherited disease is one that may be passed from generation to generation through affected genes of the sire or the dam, or sometimes through a combination of both. Genetics, the study of inheritance, is a highly complicated science, becoming increasingly so the more we learn of the subject.

There are two main problems in the control of inherited diseases in dogs. Some diseases are partly inherited, and partly occur as a result of some environmental influence, often difficult to determine precisely. The inherited element may depend on several inherited factors rather than a single gene.

Typical of this type of disease is hip dysplasia, probably the most widely known of all inherited diseases of the dog. It is a hind-leg lameness, caused by severe erosion and damage to the hip joint.

It is generally considered that inheritance accounts for about fifty

✦ BELOW
This Irish Setter is free from the distressing condition of Progressive Retinal Atrophy (PRA), which responsible breeders are doing a great deal to eliminate in the breed.

✦ LEFT
Dalmatians may be tested scientifically for deafness before they are six weeks old.

per cent of the clinical signs of hip dysplasia, and that the remainder is caused by some environmental circumstance – the dog's weight, exercise, diet, perhaps – but precisely what is not known. In these circumstances, attempts at control are slow at best, depending on diagnosis of the disease and the avoidance of affected dogs in breeding. This may sound simple but is not.

The condition affects many breeds, mostly the larger ones, including the German Shepherd. Largely due to the efforts of German Shepherd breeders, control schemes have been operating in several countries for many years now. Progress has been real but is slow, and sometimes heartbreaking for breeders, who may have used a dog and a bitch that both have excellent "hip scores", only to find that the offspring are seriously affected.

The second problem is that the disease may not show itself until the

affected animal is mature. The dog or bitch may well have been used in a breeding programme before any signs that it has the condition are seen. To some extent this may be overcome by control schemes that do not give certificates of freedom from the disease until the dogs in the scheme are old enough for the particular disease to have shown itself. Hip dysplasia is again an example: hip scoring is by an expert panel who examine X-rays of submitted dogs. These X-rays may not be taken until the dog is twelve months old.

There are several diseases that are known to be inherited in a straightforward way and are present at birth. These diseases can be controlled, depending for the success of the control scheme on the co-operation of the breeders, and their recognition that animals that show signs of the disease are actually afflicted, rather than the subject of

sale, not only for total deafness, but for partial deafness in one or both ears. There is evidence that partially deaf dogs can pass on partial or complete deafness to their offspring, and the numbers of dogs being tested are increasing rapidly in several countries. The test for dogs originated in the United States, which is probably leading the world in this area.

Almost certainly, present studies of the "genome", the genetic make-up, of all species will result in a revolution in the study and control of genetic diseases. Once the precise positions of inherited diseases on the DNA molecule are known, specific action may be taken to eliminate the problem. This approach is no longer pie in the sky. Within a very few years DNA testing will become routine.

mysterious accidents that merely mimic the condition.

The outstanding example of breeder co-operation in control of inherited disease must be the experience of Progressive Retinal Atrophy, night blindness, in Irish Setters. By the involvement of nearly all the breeders, and with recognition that the disease had a straightforward inheritance pattern, the condition has been virtually eliminated from the breed.

Up-and-coming schemes include one to control deafness in Dalmatians. For many years, a proportion of Dalmatian puppies have been born deaf or partially deaf; but breeders were generally only able to recognize stone-deaf puppies, which were put to sleep soon after birth.

Scientific testing, developed for use in people, has now enabled breeders to have their puppies examined before

NEUTERING

The advantages of neutering both male and female dogs far outweigh the possible disadvantages, and overcome the specific problems associated with either sex. Neutered males do not wander, and neutered females do not come into season.

Fewer owners in Britain neuter their dogs than in America, where the operation is as routine as neutering cats in Britain. It is noticeable also that fewer male dogs than females are neutered. Females, of course, are at risk of having a litter.

Both dogs and bitches may be neutered at the age of about six months, and it is not necessary to wait until a bitch has had a first season before having her spayed. To a considerable extent, the earlier the dog is neutered, the less complicated the operation. Early neutering does not result in failure of the dog to mature

mentally; all the dogs bred by the Guide Dogs For The Blind Association are neutered before they reach the age of six months. There are several disadvantages to neutering. After dogs of some breeds have been neutered their coats become heavier and fluffy. This happens to breeds such as the Irish Setter and the Cocker Spaniel, both of whom have naturally silky coats. The extent of the problem varies. In some dogs it may be necessary to trim the coat.

A problem that may be associated with spaying the bitch is the development of urinary incontinence

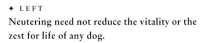
◆ LEFT
Neutering need not reduce the vitality or the zest for life of any dog.

in later life. This problem is easily cured by hormone replacement therapy, but it would still be sensible to discuss this possible problem with your veterinary surgeon before the operation. A research project currently underway may provide an answer. The problem does not occur after castration of the male.

Dogs and bitches often put on weight after being neutered. This need not happen. Dietary investigations suggest that neutered dogs have a lower nutritional requirement than entire (un-neutered) animals, possibly by as much as fifteen per cent. To avoid a dog putting on weight after it has been neutered, simply reduce its daily food ration. As with any weight-control regime, it is much easier to prevent the weight going on than to take it off once it's there. Weigh the dog regularly for a time after the neutering operation, until you have established that its weight is steady.

If you intend to keep more than one dog in your house, the situation is somewhat different. Two animals of opposite sexes will tend to live more easily together than two of the same, other than when the bitch comes into season. Two dogs kept together will tend to sort out their dominance once and for all, but two entire bitches are quite likely never to sort out their arguments, with problems tending to arise whenever one of them is coming into season.

Once you start to keep larger numbers you are likely to come across dominance problems that will have to be sorted out. Neutering has some effect on the control of dominance problems but should not be looked upon as the complete answer.

◆ RIGHT
One of the few genuine disadvantages of neutering is that it could cause the beautiful glossy coat of this Cocker Spaniel to become coarse and fluffy.

ALTERNATIVE MEDICINE

Modern conventional veterinary medicine is science based. It depends on research that produces repeatable results in the hands of competent scientific investigators, and it is subject to a considerable measure of official control with respect to safety and efficacy. The science-based approach to illness is essentially that of treating the root cause of the disease itself. Critics of this approach worry that too little attention is given to possible side-effects of potent medicines.

Holistic medical practitioners, typified by homoeopathic doctors and veterinary surgeons, regard the symptoms as essentially the reaction of the animal's body to the disease. They aim to treat the whole animal, rather than the symptoms of the disease alone.

Some alternative therapies are difficult to assess scientifically.

HOMOEOPATHIC REMEDIES

Arnica – bruising, shock and after injury

Belladonna – aggressive behaviour, ear problems and acne

Cantharis – cystitis and kidney problems

Cocculus – travel sickness

Gelsemium – nervousness and timidity

Nux Vom – digestive upsets

Pulsatilla – irregular seasons

Rhus Tox – arthritis and rheumatism

Scutellaria – nervousness, apprehension and excitability

Sulphur – skin conditions

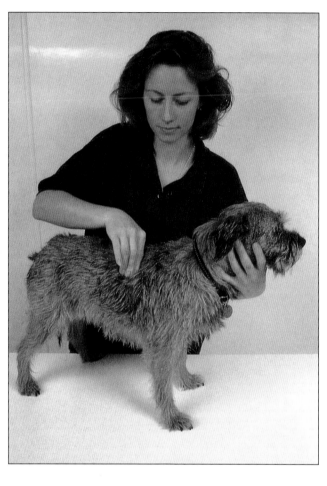

◆ LEFT
Osteopathy may produce more satisfactory long-term results in musculo-skeletal problems in dogs than the continuous use of corticosteroids, with their risk of side effects.

For instance, the holistic approach may require an animal, with apparently the same set of symptoms as another, to be treated differently because it is perceived by the practitioner to have a different basic temperament.

HOMOEOPATHY

Homoeopathy is based on an ancient medical practice of treating "like with like". There are three basic principles:

1 A medicine that in large doses produces the symptoms of a disease will in small doses cure that disease.
2 By extreme dilution the medicine's curative properties are enhanced, and all the poisonous side effects are lost.
3 Homoeopathic medicines are prescribed by the study of the whole individual and according to basic temperament.

Conventional veterinary surgeons acknowledge that all side-effects are removed in extreme dilutions, and to that extent, homoeopathic medicines are safe. Many argue that to be safe, if ineffective, by reason of the absence of any therapeutic substance is a spurious safety. Despite reservations about homoeopathy, it is almost certainly the most widely applied form of alternative therapy.

Homoeopathic remedies are invariably given by mouth, including the homoeopathic equivalent of vaccines, known as "nosodes". The medicines are either in tablet or powder form, with no unpleasant taste.

A few veterinary surgeons use homoeopathy exclusively, while a number use it regularly as part of their armoury of treatment. They tend to select cases that they consider likely to respond better to homoeopathy than to conventional medicine, often the more chronic conditions in which conventional treatments can only suppress the symptoms, sometimes with undesirable side-effects.

Veterinary surgeons using homoeopathic medicine are usually known to their colleagues locally, who will happily refer patients to the appropriate practice on request.

ACUPUNCTURE

Acupuncture is another form of treatment with roots going back thousands of years. The practice originated in China.

Treatment involves the insertion of fine needles into the skin of the patient along what are known as "meridians", which bear no relationship to recognized nerve tracks. Application of the needles reduces pain considerably, sometimes to the extent that surgery can be carried out without the patient experiencing discomfort.

Although for many years it was assumed by western doctors that the effect was purely psychological, acupuncture appears to have definite analgesic properties in animals, rather giving the lie to the "purely psychological" claim.

Many dogs seem remarkably tolerant of the application of acupuncture needles, and there is a considerable body of empirical evidence that it can have a beneficial effect on musculo-skeletal problems in dogs, as well as a less documented effect on other chronic diseases.

Acupuncture is a whole system of medicine in Chinese tradition, but in western veterinary medicine it's used as an auxiliary to other more conventional treatments.

There are few associations of veterinary acupuncturists, and practitioners of this skill in veterinary medicine are relatively uncommon. There are, however, sufficient vets with an interest in acupuncture to make it worthwhile asking your own veterinary surgeon for help if the occasion arises.

HERBALISM

Herbalism has probably the longest tradition of any system of medicine known to man. Plants have been used for their medicinal properties since time immemorial, and they have provided the basis of the modern pharmaceutical industry's research programmes since its foundation. Many modern drugs are derived from plant products.

It is inevitable that with a practice as steeped in antiquity as herbalism, different traditions have grown up in different parts of the world. For instance, there is a Chinese tradition, and Islamic influences in western herbalism are clearly marked.

Herbalists differ from conventional therapists in their use of the whole plant, or unrefined extracts of parts of the plant, rather than specific chemical entities isolated from the plant.

The best-known illustration of this difference in approach is the use of the foxglove plant. The foxglove (*Digitalis*

Liquorice root has mild laxative properties.

purpurea) was discovered to have a beneficial effect on some of the symptoms of heart disease many hundreds of years ago. An extract of the plant has been in use since the eighteenth century, but it has always been recognized as being dangerous in

COMMON HERBAL REMEDIES

Buchu – diuretic and urinary antiseptic
Cascara – laxative, bitter tonic
Cayenne – circulatory stimulant
Dandelion – liver problems
Elderberry – rheumatism, anaemia
Eucalyptus – bronchitis
Garlic – infections, worm infestations
Liquorice – anti-inflammatory, mild laxative
Peppermint – colic, travel sickness
Raspberry – reproductive problems
Rhubarb – constipation and diarrhoea
Skullcap – hysteria, anxiety
Valerian – colic, travel sickness, behavioural problems

overdosage. Pharmaceutical chemists were able to isolate active elements in foxglove extracts, which enabled them more accurately to prescribe the drugs for control of heart disease. But Digitalis, the original extract of foxglove, still has its adherents in medical practice, who prefer it to the more refined alternatives, suspecting that the process of refinement has removed some part of the efficacy of the original.

Compared with conventional medicine, herbalists have, once again, a more holistic approach, preferring to treat the whole animal rather than a specific disease.

Despite the holistic approach of the veterinary herbalists, some of their preparations have become so well established that they are regarded almost as conventional medicines. One remedy, available in Europe, with remarkable powers is rescue cream. This is a general salve that soothes and

The leaves of the peppermint plant are mainly used for their effect on the digestive tract.

Skullcap is a calming herbal remedy.

restores damaged skin. Its efficacy is at least comparable with many restricted, prescription-only skin preparations.

There are very few veterinary herbalists, but some countries have an official institute of medical herbalists, which could put you in touch with a practitioner.

AROMATHERAPY

Aromatherapy could be regarded as an offshoot of herbalism, in that the system uses extracts from plants, prepared as the essential oils of those plants, as a form of therapy. The oils are used either for massage or simply inhaled by a diffusion into the air, and are considered to be useful for a wide range of ailments. Aromatherapy is rarely used by veterinary surgeons, although some owners are sufficiently knowledgeable to be able to use the therapy as an adjunct to conventional medicine.

OSTEOPATHY

Veterinary osteopathy is now well established as a supportive therapy in veterinary medicine.

Osteopathy, as originally understood, held that most or all diseases are caused by displacement of bones and are curable by manipulation. It is doubtful if any practising osteopaths now adhere totally to this doctrine, but there is no doubt that manipulation can effect considerable improvement in a number of chronic-disease conditions. Musculo-skeletal problems in the dog seem to be particularly responsive to osteopathic manipulation. As with the insertion of acupuncture needles, dogs seem to tolerate osteopathy remarkably well, although some naturally unruly dogs may need sedation before treatment.

PHYSIOTHERAPY

Physiotherapists have long had an association with conventional medicine. Their approach is more scientifically based than traditional osteopaths, and their training and work is medically supervised. Physiotherapy treats illness by physical measures. It includes massage and manipulation, in which respect it is like osteopathy, but also uses heat, electricity, and passive or active exercise. It aims to restore the functions of joints and muscles.

Many physiotherapists are involved in veterinary medicine, but there is no specific association. Veterinary surgeons will usually know of a local physiotherapist with an interest in veterinary work, and will invariably be happy to refer a patient. Fractured legs on the mend often respond well to physiotherapy, which stimulates muscles and tendons that have tended to waste or lose their strength during the period of bone healing. Physiotherapy may be used in any circumstances where gentle manipulation is likely to improve mobility.

DOGS AND HUMAN HEALTH

There are some diseases that may affect both dogs and humans. The technical term for such a disease is "zoonosis".

The most feared of these diseases is undoubtedly **rabies**, the reason for long-standing quarantine laws between the United Kingdom and all other countries, which have only recently been changed. The laws throughout the EU countries have now been dramatically relaxed for many domestic pets. It is now possible to acquire a "pet passport", which allows owners to bring their pet into Britain without them spending six months in quarantine kennels, as the old laws used to require.

The passport requirements are very stringent and include a full healthcheck by a vet, which includes up-to-date immunizations against rabies and many other diseases. Animals must also have an identification chip inserted, a photo, current certificates and pet insurance.

When travelling in an area that is not rabies-free, consult a doctor immediately if you are bitten by a dog or any other animal.

Fleas, common on dogs – most frequently actually the cat flea – will bite humans. It is unlikely that dog or cat fleas can survive on humans, so a few intensely itchy bites are the only likely problem. The presence of flea bites on you or your children is a timely reminder that flea control on your dog has, perhaps, not been as effective as you thought.

Rabbit mites frequently cause a skin rash in dogs. They are capable of biting humans, and may cause an itchy rash on the forearms from contact with the affected dog. The rash is unlikely to spread.

Ringworm is not a common disease in dogs but, when it does occur, precautions should be taken to avoid its spread to human members of the family. It is a true zoonosis and can establish itself on the human skin. Affected areas are again likely to be those of contact – the hands and forearms.

Toxocara, the most frequently encountered roundworm in puppies, and indeed almost universal in very young puppies, has been implicated in a rare specific type of eye disease in children. Roundworms that are ingested by a species other than their normal host may encyst and settle in almost any part of the body, but are known to

◆ LEFT
Dogs should never be permitted to run freely where children may play because of the risk that they may deposit faeces.

◆ BELOW LEFT
Owners must always collect faeces deposited by their dogs.

◆ BELOW RIGHT
Many local authorities now provide dog litter bins. They are to be encouraged.

invade the eye. These cysts have been known to cause blindness. Such an accident is extremely rare but, of course, a tragedy for the child and his or her parents if it happens.

Good hygiene and vigilance should prevent any child from coming in contact with dog faeces. Puppies must be wormed regularly, every three weeks until they are six months old. Their faeces must be collected, at home as well as on the street, and the puppy should be taught to defecate in a prescribed spot in the garden, not in a public place. If an accident does happen while you are out exercising your dog, scoop it up. Always go prepared. Legislation now covers fouling by dogs in public places, and "poop scoop" laws are in force in many areas.

Simple hygiene for children must be practised: children should always wash their hands after playing with a dog. But children should not be discouraged from having contact with dogs – there is so much to be gained from a happy association between child and dog that, provided risks are minimized by adopting sensible precautions, their close companionship should be encouraged. Remember, the dog is our oldest friend.

◆ BELOW LEFT
Dogs should be discouraged from playing with the baby's toys.

INDEX

PHOTOGRAPHER'S ACKNOWLEDGEMENTS
I would like to express my thanks to the breeders, and to C. Fry, L. Graham, M. Peacock, S. Bradley, A. Wells, P. Beaven, J. & P. Canning, L. & A. Piatneuer, V. Dyer, B. Stnet and J. Hay. Thanks also to Pampered Pets of Godalming, Colin Clarke Veterinary Practice, Celia Cross Greyhound Rescue, Canine Partners for Independence and Weycolour Limited. Last but not least. thanks to my partner Alison Hay for her administration and assistance.